CONSTITUTIONAL LAW
AND LIABILITY FOR
PUBLIC-SECTOR POLICE

Airports
Port Authorities
Public Medical Facilities
Public Colleges and Universities

By

Dan S. Murrell, J.D., LL.M.
Cecil C. Humphreys School of Law
Memphis State University
Memphis, Tennessee 38152

and

William O. Dwyer, Ph.D.
Center for Applied Psychological Research
Department of Psychology
Memphis State University
Mcmphis, Tennessee 38152

Carolina Academic Press
Durham, North Carolina

ACKNOWLEDGEMENTS

The authors are very grateful for the help of all those law enforcement officers, attorneys, graduate students, and others who assisted us with advice, suggestions, and counsel during the development of this work. Specifically, we are indebted to Richard Furr, Inspector for Field Operations, Office of Security and Law Enforcement, Department of Veterans' Affairs; James Welna, Chief, Minneapolis-St. Paul Metropolitan Airports Commission Police Department; Gene Sheridan, Commander, Minneapolis-St. Paul Metropolitan Airports Commission Police Department; Robert Hewlett, Assistant Chief, University of Tennessee Medical Center Police Department; Keith Benich, Chief, Nashville Metropolitan Airport Police Department; Sgt. Joseph Murphy, Training Officer, Nashville Metropolitan Airport Police Department; and Roger Fowler, Director, Department of Public Safety, Memphis State University for their excellent comments, suggestions, and evaluations concerning the content of this book.

We wish to especially thank Lisa Coleman for her assistance in research, and Susan Vazquez for her help in editing the manuscript.

ISBN 0-89089-502-3
LC Number 92-71442
Copyright 1992 Dan S. Murrell and William O. Dwyer

Printed in the United States of America

TO ORDER COPIES, CONTACT:
Carolina Academic Press
700 Kent Street
Durham, North Carolina 27701
(919)489-7486   FAX (919)493-5668

TO THE READER------

This book is intended to help you, the reader, but we also need your help to insure that it meets your needs. If you have any suggestions, questions, problems, or situations that need to be addressed, please let us know so that we may consider those problems for future editions. We will try to respond individually to your correspondence.

We would like to know about your particular jurisdiction's laws, statutes, and regulations and will address those whenever possible in the future.

Any correspondence should be sent to either of the authors:

Professor Dan S. Murrell
Cecil C. Humphreys School of Law
Memphis State University
Memphis, Tennessee 38152
(901) 678-3219

or

Professor William O. Dwyer
Center for Applied Psychological Research
Department of Psychology
Memphis State University
Memphis, Tennessee 38152
(901) 678-2149

NOTE: Blank pages have been left at appropriate intervals for your notes and questions.

TABLE OF CONTENTS

TABLE OF CASES

CHAPTER 1

INTRODUCTION

As part of the evolution of American law enforcement, there has been a significant increase in the employment of police in public-sector institutions such as airports, state colleges and universities, public hospitals, port authorities, and medical centers. Often these police have replaced private security systems which have proved insufficient to meet continually increasing needs for law enforcement and maintenance of public safety. Although these police are in the public sector and often receive the same training as municipal and state police, they must function in a unique setting, with significant exposure to the public, and with consistent pressure to be sensitive to the public-relations aspects of the job as they interact with patrons and other employees. Like officers in other settings, police in public-sector institutions must abide by constitutional guidelines and mandates in their encounters with the public. As is the case for other officers, if institutional police violate these guidelines in their dealings with the public, they face the potential consequences of suppressed evidence as well as personal criminal and civil liability.

The purpose of this book is to provide a quick and handy reference for police officers employed by public entities about how the Constitution, as interpreted through various court decisions, as well as liability considerations, influence their contacts with the public. The general rules are essentially the same as they would be for any police officer; yet these institutional police operate in a unique environment that sometimes makes the application of case law somewhat difficult and confusing, but may also give them more latitude in policing. Our intention is to provide a sound framework against which the practice of public-institution law enforcement may be measured. The book is not meant to be a complete list of "Do's and Don'ts" because various state laws and local regulations, as well as agency guidelines and procedures, may also have a bearing on the breadth of enforcement authority given institutional police officers. Therefore, where more restrictive guidelines are in place, the reader is cautioned to make a note of them and abide by them.

NOTES

CHAPTER 2

LIABILITY AND CIVIL RIGHTS

A. BACKGROUND

When people make use of public institutions such as airports, colleges and universities, ports of authority, and medical complexes, they bring with them an assumption that these agencies were created by the taxpayers to serve the needs of the public. From this belief comes a general expectation of personal liberty and freedom from unnecessary interference by agents of authority. Thus, public institution police managers speak in terms of "low-key" law enforcement: doing the least possible to gain compliance with laws and regulations. On the other hand, the public also brings with it an "expectation of security and privacy"; people expect, perhaps even demand, to be safe in their persons and their property. If loss or injury to the public is reasonably foreseeable by management, a host of recent court cases suggest that management must act to remedy the problem. And yet, if in its zeal to protect the people and physical resources, law enforcement unnecessarily impinges on individuals' civil rights or their expectations of privacy, the public is certain to seek remedy for what it perceives as a violation of its prerogatives.

Unlike most other police officers, public-sector institutional police serve as guardians over the people and areas in which they enforce the law, a condition that places on them a unique set of expectations from the public. Also unlike other law enforcement officers, public institution police are often exposed to increased administrative and political remedies which may be used by members of the public who feel that they were mistreated. All these factors add up to a requirement for the professional and temperate use of police powers in public institutions. Of the various means that have been created for guaranteeing the protection of the public's constitutional rights, criminal and civil liability are of the greatest concern to officers and administrators.

3

Although the Supreme Court has held that law enforcement officers enjoy a certain "qualified good-faith immunity" from liability for their actions, they may still be held criminally and civilly liable if they act outside the scope of their employment, violate their agency's guidelines, or violate a person's civil rights.

B. CRIMINAL LIABILITY

Federal as well as state statutes make it a criminal offense for anyone acting in the capacity of a public law enforcement officer to willfully violate an individual's civil rights that are guaranteed by the United States Constitution or federal law. For example, Title 18 of the United States Code, Section 242, makes it illegal for an officer acting under color of law to willfully subject any inhabitant of a state, territory or district to the "deprivation of any rights, privileges or immunities secured or protected by the Constitution or laws of the United States..." Police officers who willfully and with specific intent violate someone's civil rights may be convicted of a crime and imprisoned. For this to occur, they would have to be proven guilty beyond a reasonable doubt.

C. CIVIL LIABILITY

Federal as well as state governments have established provisions for people who have been deprived of their civil rights by officers acting under color of law to sue those officers in civil court for compensation for any losses (including losses of a right) or harm which may have resulted from the deprivation. Title 42, Section 1983 of the U.S. Code, for example, states that anyone acting under color of law who "subjects, or causes to be subjected, any citizen of the United States or other person within the jurisdiction thereof to the deprivation of any rights, privileges or immunities secured by the Constitution and laws, shall be liable to the party injured in an action at law, lawsuit in equity, or other proper proceeding for redress." To be successful in such a suit, a plaintiff would not have to prove willfulness on the part of the officer, and the level of proof required is merely "a preponderance of the evidence" and not "beyond a reasonable doubt."

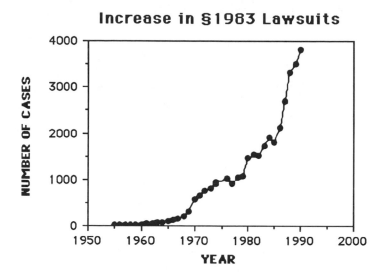

Increase in §1983 Lawsuits

Number of §1983 cases in the federal courts from 1955 through 1990

5

NOTES

CHAPTER 3

REVIEW OF POLICE POWERS

A. THE CONSTITUTION AND POLICE AUTHORITY

In the last thirty years, the Supreme Court has energetically articulated (and restricted) the latitude within which law enforcement officers may exercise their police authority. The Court's decisions have had a significant impact on most aspects of police activity. Most of these decisions have had their foundations in the first eight of the Ten Amendments, known as the Bill of Rights. Of the 23 rights guaranteed in these eight Amendments, 12 have a direct bearing on criminal procedure, and of these, the Fourth, Fifth, and Sixth Amendments are the most relevant for public sector law enforcement.

The **Fourth Amendment** (1) protects people against unreasonable searches and seizures, and (2) restricts the conditions under which warrants may be issued. The **Fifth Amendment** (1) requires a grand jury in criminal cases, (2) protects against double jeopardy, and (3) prohibits a person from being forced to testify against himself or herself. The **Sixth Amendment** addresses the rights of individuals in criminal prosecutions: (1) the right to a speedy and public trial, (2) the right to an impartial jury, (3) the right to be informed of the charges against the defendant, (4) the right to subpoena witnesses, (5) the right to confront the accuser, and (6) the right to counsel.

Although the **First Amendment** does not bear directly on criminal procedure as such, it does guarantee five specific rights, two of which are quite relevant to law enforcement activities in public institutions: (1) freedom of speech, and (2) freedom of peaceable assembly. This amendment may also protect an individual's right to freely exercise his or her religion.

7

What follows in this book is an elaboration of how the courts' interpretations of some of these rights have established the limits on what you, as a police officer in a public institution, are able to do as an agent of authority.

B. OFFICER AUTHORITY

What are police powers?

Police powers are inherent in the state governmental function and are granted to the federal government by the United States Constitution; they provide the authority and responsibility for designated governmental agents to provide for peace and order, to enforce the law, to detain and arrest others, and to seize property as evidence pursuant to knowledge of the commission of some crime.

What is the difference between the arrest power of citizens and that of public law enforcement officers?

Citizens possess the right to arrest perpetrators of crimes, but if after such an arrest, it is determined that the arrestee did not commit the crime, or the state does not prosecute, the arresting citizen may be liable for false arrest. On the other hand, a law enforcement officer employed by a public entity has certain immunities from such liability because, unlike the citizen who must have absolute knowledge (unless given special statutory authority) that the person to be arrested actually committed the crime, all that is required of a law enforcement officer (i.e., a person who is operating under color of law) is that he or she had probable cause to believe that a crime was committed and the person arrested committed it. Minor variations may exist among different jurisdictions.

What is "good-faith immunity"?

Historically, officers of the sovereign were given immunity under the theory that the sovereign could do no wrong. Today courts continue to recognize that, in order to do their jobs effectively, law enforcement officers require a certain amount of immunity from the consequences of their actions. This immunity, however, is qualified; it requires that the officer be acting in good faith. Like many concepts in law, "good faith" does not have an official definition, but in general terms, it refers to an officer's behaving in a reasonable manner that is based on a reasonable level of training and skills possession. In other words, it is not enough merely for you to think that you are doing right. Your actions must meet the standard of what a reasonable and adequately trained officer would be likely to do in the situation. Of course, in the last analysis, a jury will make that judgment if the matter is contested in court.

What is "probable cause"?

Probable cause refers to a level of certainty. It means you must have more reason to believe than not that a particular person committed a particular crime, or that evidence of a crime is in a particular place.

Who is operating under "color of law"?

For the purpose of exercising police authority, any person who is (or has the appearance of being) employed by a public entity for the purpose of enforcing laws, supervising those enforcing laws, regulations or ordinances, preventing and detecting crime, and apprehending criminals is working under color of law. This would include commissioned police hired by public airports, colleges and universities, hospitals, or any other public institution. It would not ordinarily include private security guards, even though their duty posts may include public institutions.

Some jurisdictions employ uniformed personnel who appear to be officers but are not "commissioned," and who serve in such capacities as traffic directors, issuers of parking tickets, etc. For purposes of constitutional guarantees regarding arrest, search and seizure, and other civil rights, these officers are probably acting under color of law. Similarly, agencies that employ uniformed personnel on an unarmed, non-commissioned basis until they have completed law enforcement training are normally placing them under the mantle of color of law, a status that has definite implications in terms of criminal and civil liability (e.g., 18 U.S.C. §242 and 42 U.S.C. §1983 could be bases for liability). It may also give them some protection under the sovereign immunity umbrella.

The general rule is that if, through your appearance, talk or actions, you appear to the public to have police authority, then you are probably acting under color of law. This is true whether or not you have been given statutory or administrative authority to enforce the law.

What is the difference between a police officer with a law enforcement commission and one who does not have a commission?

When a public entity commissions an individual as a law enforcement officer, it is granting that officer the additional authority to enforce the laws and provides limited immunity when the officer is acting under color of law. This may include the authority to carry a weapon, effect arrests, conduct investigations, serve warrants, and carry out related police functions. It also imposes on the officer the duties and responsibilities inherent in the commission.

What is the significance of being a "sworn" law enforcement officer?

In terms of your status with regard to color of law or your law enforcement authority, whether or not you were "sworn in" as a law enforcement officer has little bearing on your discretion or your authority. The issue is whether you were hired directly by the public entity to enforce the law and prevent, detect, and investigate crime.

Who has the authority to exercise police powers under color of law?

Authority refers to what you can properly do as a law enforcement officer. It is granted either through specific state or federal statutes or, in some cases, through common law. It is essential that you be familiar with the source and the scope of your authority as a police officer.

What if I hold law enforcement commissions from more than one jurisdiction?

As an example, you are an airport police officer, and you have also been commissioned by the local sheriff to assist in enforcing state narcotics laws in the area. Or, in your spare time you serve as a volunteer reserve police officer for a local community. Holding multiple commissions means that you have been given police authority to enforce the relevant laws and regulations of the various jurisdictions that commissioned you. It is, however, not a guarantee that, should you become exposed to criminal or civil liability as a result of your police actions, those other jurisdictions will provide for your defense or pay any judgments against you. This very important point is often not clearly understood by officers in such situations. Because of potential problems, multiple commissions should normally be avoided.

C. JURISDICTION

What is jurisdiction?

Jurisdiction normally refers to a specific territory over which a sovereign governmental entity legally exercises authority. It is usually articulated (restricted or expanded) in statutory language. Jurisdiction in criminal matters either exists or it does not, and it may never be waived. Regarding any law of a particular jurisdiction, a person either violated it or did not. Officers, therefore, either have the legal authority to act or they do not, and could easily become criminally and civilly liable for kidnapping, false imprisonment, robbery, etc., if they exercise police powers without appropriate jurisdictional authority. Whereas authority refers to *what* you may do, jurisdiction refers to where a crime is committed. You should be familiar with your jurisdiction and avoid acting outside of it.

What are the jurisdictional issues related to discipline vs. criminal prosecution?

In some institutional settings, inappropriate behavior may be dealt with by either criminal prosecution or disciplinary procedures. Officers desiring criminal prosecution are bound by the traditional constitutional limitations. Disciplinary procedures, on the other hand, allow the officer expanded inquiry and response determined by institutional purposes and needs and are generally permitted because of consent or contract. For example, a student found drinking an alcoholic beverage in a public university prohibiting such activity may be dealt with through criminal prosecution or through disciplinary procedures, or both. Or, airport police could, in lieu of prosecution, suspend an employee's driving privileges in the airport operations area, if that employee were caught violating driving regulations and procedures.

What if I intervene in some criminal activity outside of my agency's jurisdiction and outside the normal scope of my authority?

For example, what if an airport police officer intervenes in the robbery of a local service station? It is important that you understand your particular state's law on this issue. Some states convey the status of "peace officer" on all law enforcement personnel, and expect all officers to intervene, especially in a felony. Other states do not have such a law, and you would be acting as a citizen should you become involved (unless, of course, it was at the specific request of an officer with the proper authority). Regardless of the particular authority conferred on you in such situations, you should have the answer to two very important questions: (1) If my actions lead to some criminal or civil liability, who is going to pay for my defense? (2) If there is a financial judgment against me, who is going to pay the judgment?

It is important to understand that the insurance carrier that wrote your agency's policy to cover liability may not provide you with any protection unless your activity as an officer was necessary to the operation or functioning of your agency. Your intervention in some law enforcement action outside your jurisdiction may not fall under their definition of "necessary." The same may be true if your agency is self-insured. For this reason, many institutions do not allow their officers to carry off-duty weapons around the community, even if allowed by state law.

If I am in uniform, do I still have my citizen's arrest powers?

Here again, you must become familiar with the laws of your particular state. In some states uniformed law enforcement officers give up their citizen's arrest powers. In most jurisdictions you have your police powers whether in or out of uniform.

D. LAWS AND REGULATIONS

Police officers in public institutions may be given the responsibility of enforcing both laws and regulations, sometimes of more than one jurisdiction.

What are criminal laws?

Criminal Laws designate certain acts or failures to act as being illegal and provide specific punishments for them. To be enacted, laws must be passed by either state or federal legislatures (depending upon jurisdiction) or have uncontested common law existence at the state level.

What are regulations?

Regulations may also articulate limits on behavior and may carry penalties of fines and imprisonment. Unlike laws, however, regulations are not specifically enacted by a legislature; rather they are promulgated by an agency (e.g., the Department of the Interior, F.A.A. or a state university). Of course, the agency depends on legislation for its right to promulgate such regulations. Regulations can have the force and effectiveness of law; that is, their violation can lead to legal action, arrest, fines, and imprisonment. Governmental entities often operate under special legislative enactments and will decree special rules and regulations that will usually give additional authority to its police personnel.

What about special consent or contracts affecting people who want to use the institution's facilities?

The authority flowing from regulations is often couched in terms of consent, direct or implied. The consent may create the additional authority through the forfeiture of some constitutional right or some degree of privacy on the part of the public utilizing the facility. Examples are airports, public colleges and universities, ports of authority and public hospitals. For instance, air travel is a privilege, and one forfeits a degree of privacy and the constitutional protection against searches if one wishes to fly. The protected interest is safety for the public in general.

Other institutions may rely on contracts. Colleges and universities, for example, may rely on similar expanded authority and restrictions on conduct. A student may agree, in a contract with a university, for example, to open his or her room to police in exchange for being permitted to attend the school or drive through or live on campus.

Institutional police officers routinely have additional authority to deal with the necessities of their institution. This authority generally takes the form of determining if people on the facility have a legitimate right of access and interests compatible with the purpose of the institution. It may, there-

14

fore, allow intrusions into privacy to check identification, purpose of the visit, destination, and in some instances, permit a search of the persons, the items in their possession, and their vehicle.

E. DEADLY FORCE

RULE OF LAW: Deadly force may not be used to effect an arrest. It may be used only to protect yourself or others from imminent lethal force or severe injury.

For all public-sector police, the question of when deadly force may be employed is fairly simple to answer; it may be applied only in defense of the officer's life or someone else's. Until 1985 some states allowed officers to shoot to stop fleeing felons. Since 1985, however, the Supreme Court has ruled that shooting a fleeing felon merely to prevent escape is a violation of civil rights.

Under what conditions may I use deadly force?

Specifically, the Supreme Court restricted the use of deadly force to situations of (1) defense of the officer's life, (2) defense of others' lives, or (3) when the officer has probable cause to believe that the suspect has committed a violent crime involving the infliction or threat of death or serious harm, or probable cause to believe that the suspect is armed and poses an imminent substantial risk to others. To be protected by qualified good faith immunity, you must follow the established deadly force policy of your agency, and if you are using deadly force (in accordance with policy) to stop a person under condition (3) above, you must exhaust all other reasonable means of apprehension and, whenever possible, identify yourself and warn suspects that if they do not stop you will use deadly force.

15

NOTES

CHAPTER 4

CONFRONTING A SUSPICIOUS PERSON

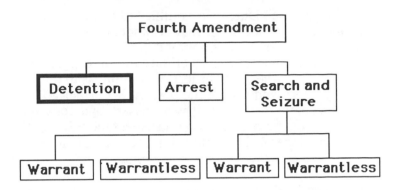

RULE OF LAW: You may stop an individual, even though you do not have an adequate cause for arrest, if you observe unusual behavior or circumstances which lead you to suspect that criminal activity may be occurring, has occurred or is about to occur, or if you believe that the person may be involved in injury to the facility or in violation of the institution's regulations. The stop is to allow you to confirm or eliminate your suspicions concerning the illegal activity.

For institutional purposes, you may stop an individual to determine his or her right to be present on the protected premises and expel or arrest those who do not wish to be identified or challenged.

A. STOPPING AN INDIVIDUAL

When conducting a stop you must identify yourself or be identifiable as a law enforcement officer. As an institutional police officer, you may have a broader latitude to make a stop than do most other conventional officers, because of the institution's interests and needs (e.g., the necessity for more

17

rules and regulations). Of course, you must act with the discretion of a reasonable, good-faith officer concerned with the public's safety and the institution's security.

1. **Routine stops**: During a routine stop you may ask people about their conduct or that of others relative to your institutional concern, and you may detain individuals for a brief, but reasonable time, to facilitate the investigation or inquiry. You may check identification, inquire as to destination and purpose, and search the person, his or her possessions, and vehicle if you feel it is necessary and consistent with institutional guidelines, or you suspect the person may be carrying illegal objects, prohibited items, or materials dangerous to the institution or its personnel.

You may also hold items that were in possession of the person detained (e.g., a knife, a backpack, a briefcase, etc.) for the duration of a reasonable stop.

You may stop suspicious people, whether they are on foot, on bikes, in vehicles, boats or other conveyances.

You may also observe all items in plain view during the stop and may seize any evidence, fruits, or instrumentalities of any crime. This observation may be aided by a flashlight beam. What you observe, hear, and smell during the stop may be used to help develop probable cause for an arrest or a search warrant.

When may I stop and question an individual whose behavior or presence seems questionable?

In order to stop and question an individual about possible illegal activity, you must have a **reasonable suspicion** that a crime has been, is being, or is about to be committed and that the person is somehow connected with it. Reasonable suspicion involves articulable facts or apparent facts that would lead a reasonable and prudent officer to believe that a crime may be taking place and that the suspicious person is involved. It must be more than a "hunch" or a "feeling" but

18

does not necessarily have to meet the requirement of probable cause.

If you wish to stop a person because his or her presence in the facility seems questionable, you must, likewise, have a valid concern about the appropriateness of the person's presence or activity. For example, in some facilities, reasonable suspicion could be invoked because the person is not displaying a required identification card.

Mere suspicion, based on your sense or feeling for a situation, may cause you to make inquiries of a person, but gives you no authority to compel a stop, force someone to answer you, or even to conduct a "Terry" type frisk. In order to detain and frisk someone, you must have reasonable suspicion.

In an investigative stop, does a suspect have to answer my questions?

No. People are under no legal obligation to answer any of your questions. If they refuse to talk to you, you may NOT use this refusal as a reason to arrest. In other words, the exercise of a civil right cannot be used to help establish probable cause. For example, you are on patrol at night and you see someone walking alone in a university building. You ask him if he needs help and he says "No." You become suspicious and ask him his name and what he is doing. He tells you that it's none of your business. Without any other information, you cannot arrest him, nor can you force him to answer. If, however, you see that he has blood on his shirt or is carrying an unauthorized weapon, etc., you may continue the stop a reasonable amount of time for further investigation. As a reminder, a person may always be ejected from a place where he or she has no right to be.

You may also check identification, inquire as to destination and purpose, and search the person, his or her possessions and vehicle if you feel it is necessary *and consistent with written institutional guidelines*, because the person may be carrying illegal objects, prohibited items, or materials dangerous to the institution or its personnel. If the individual fails to respond and permit the necessary inquiry or search, that is an adequate basis to expel the person from the premises.

For example, if a campus police officer encounters a male walking in the hall of a women's residence hall at 2:00 A.M., the officer may be justified in stopping the individual, inquiring into his business. If the officer determines that his presence is inappropriate, he or she may, as a minimum, expel the individual from the residence hall and, if warranted, take the individual into custody. Likewise, a person found without surgical attire in a sterile section of a hospital could similarly be dealt with. The same would also be true for an individual without apparent identification and found by airport police within the airport operations area.

2. **Roadblocks**: Roadblocks may be used in certain situations to search vehicles going through a particular point. As an example, a roadblock could be used to search all vehicles exiting a medical complex for the purpose of looking for a missing child. A roadblock may be used for systematic and directed checks of permits, licenses, etc. You should not look where you are not likely to find the object of the search. When the sought item or person is found, the roadblock should be dismantled.

The unique character of your security function at your type of facility will allow you to operate routine checkpoints to enter the institution, and allow you to check identification, inquire as to destination and purpose, and search the person, his or her possessions and vehicle if you feel it is necessary and consistent with institutional guidelines, because the person may be carrying illegal objects, or prohibited items or materials dangerous to the institution or its personnel. You may prevent entry if the person fails to qualify or cooperate.

During the stop, all items that you observe in plain view that you believe to be the evidence, fruits, or instrumentalities of a crime may be properly seized. To justify the warrantless seizure of an item in plain view, the officer must not only be lawfully located in a place from which the object can be plainly seen, but the officer must also have a lawful right or access to the object itself.

Roadblocks should be as brief and unobtrusive as possible and should last no longer than necessary to accomplish the purpose.

May I establish a roadblock to stop every vehicle to check for such things as: underage use of alcohol or invalid operator's permits?

Yes. You may establish a roadblock for specific purposes when you suspect that particular criminal activity is occurring, such as underage use of alcohol. Your roadblock should be limited to stopping those people who could be violators within the framework of your purpose. As an example, you should not stop older persons when searching for youth. The key is to keep the intrusion to a minimum. Searching for invalid operators' permits should normally be by departmental or agency plan and be very directed.

While it is not necessary, you can always seek a warrant to establish a roadblock. This judicial scrutiny of your activity satisfies the bulk of the constitutional mandates and helps to protect your actions and any evidence that may be seized.

May I establish roadblocks to stop certain classes of vehicles (e.g., pickup trucks, vans, or vehicles being driven by juveniles) to check for such things as underage alcohol use?

Yes. You may stop certain classes of vehicles so long as there is a clear purpose and not a general "fishing expedition" or arbitrary action.

May I establish a roadblock to stop every vehicle that matches the description of one used in a recent crime in the vicinity?

Yes. You may establish a roadblock stopping all vehicles, that match the description of the vehicle involved in suspected or actual criminal activity. The intrusion and delay time should always be kept to a minimum but may be of sufficient time for adequate inquiry. Once it is determined that the vehicle or occupants are not involved, the vehicle should be released and the investigation should not proceed into other areas unless plain view evidence gives rise to appropriate further inquiry. Once the object of the search, vehicle, or person is seized, the roadblock must be dismantled for that purpose, although it could be converted for other specific purposes, such as discovery of a new crime or offenders, etc.

You may also establish a roadblock stopping all vehicles with occupants, either by number or appearance, similar to those suspected of committing a crime in the area.

May I establish a roving roadblock for which I patrol along roads and stop certain classes of vehicles (e.g., pickups) to check for such things as underage alcohol use?

Yes, if the purpose matches the vehicle or its occupants as described above.

May I set up a roadblock in which I systematically stop a certain proportion of the vehicles (e.g., every fifth one) to check for such things as illegal use of alcohol, or invalid driver's licenses?

Yes, if your plan is systematic and the purpose matches the plan, or the vehicle or its occupants as described above. As a reminder, you cannot stop vehicles on an arbitrary basis. Of course, such activity should be conducted only pursuant to written guidelines to reduce the potential for abuse or exposure to liability.

While effecting a traffic stop, may I make the driver get out of the vehicle?

Yes. Without any further justification, you may routinely order the driver of a vehicle you have stopped to get out of the vehicle during your encounter. Unless public safety dictates, however, you may not order a person to re-enter the vehicle. For example, you may not order a visitor to return to the vehicle after exiting it during a traffic stop, unless it is necessary to move the vehicle. The same would generally hold true for passengers who exit the vehicle. Unless there is a clear safety need, you could not order them to get back into the vehicle.

Because of exposure to potential liabilities, it is unadvisable to place the recipient of a citation in your patrol vehicle while you are completing the citation. If the question is raised, the courts will generally construe the placing of an individual in your patrol vehicle as a arrest.

May I check the VIN during a stop at a roadblock?

Yes, you may check the VIN (vehicle identification number) during any lawful stop whether at a roadblock or not. You may reach into the vehicle and move objects covering the VIN plate, and any evidence, fruits or instrumentalities of a crime discovered in the course of such action may be properly seized. The stop, under appropriate circumstances, such as looking for a particular stolen vehicle, may even be to check the VIN number.

May I establish a roadblock/checkpoint to stop every vehicle to check for an intoxicated driver?

Yes. Usually referred to as "OUI (DWI) checkpoints," they may be legally established to allow you to briefly stop every vehicle and talk to the driver to make sure he or she is sober enough to drive.

What are the conditions and restrictions of such a checkpoint?

To make sure that your checkpoint is being conducted in a manner consistent with guidelines enumerated by the Supreme Court, you should do the following:

a. Make a public announcement (e.g., in local newspapers) that you will be conducting such stops over the next few weeks/months.

b. Establish a written policy detailing the conduct of such checkpoints.

c. Obtain written directives from management for each checkpoint occurrence, detailing exactly where, when, and for what duration the checkpoint will be conducted.

d. Establish checkpoint locations that will maximize safety for the officers and motorists. Clearly identify them with signs, traffic cones, and adequate lighting.

e. Stops should be brief and courteous, requiring only a short conversation during which the officer can look for signs of intoxication, such as presence of alcohol in vehicle, odor of an intoxicating beverage, quality of speech, general demeanor, etc.

f. If, based upon these observations, your suspicion is aroused that the driver may be intoxicated, the stop should then proceed as any other OUI (DWI) traffic stop.

g. Be sure to have adequate manpower present to handle more than one vehicle at a time, or any arrests, vehicle impoundments, etc. that may be required.

h. Do not let your checkpoint develop into a traffic jam. Drivers should not have to wait very long for you to contact them. If such a condition begins developing, it is wise to wave all of them through without contacting them.

B. FRISKING A SUSPECT

RULE OF LAW: During a stop, you may conduct a frisk to protect yourself or others if you have a reasonable suspicion that the individual stopped may be armed and dangerous.

1. Individual

A frisk of an individual is a patdown of the outer clothing for the sole purpose of looking for **weapons**. A frisk may also extend to the inside of an over garment, such as an overcoat. You may use the minimum reasonable force, excluding deadly force, necessary to compel submission to the frisk. For example, this may include the use of handcuffs if they are necessary to restrain the suspect during a frisk.

What is "reasonable force?"

Reasonable force is that amount which is minimally necessary and which would be used by a reasonable and prudent officer to gain compliance from a suspect. Any amount of force above this level would be considered **punishment** and would, therefore, be excessive.

When may I frisk an individual whom I have stopped?

You may frisk suspects whom you have stopped only if you have a **reasonable** (that is, articulable) suspicion that they may be armed and that they may harm you or others. You do not need probable cause, but neither is a "hunch" or a "feeling" sufficient. Reasonable suspicion for a frisk is established essentially by a combination of the suspect's demeanor and the bulkiness of the clothing being worn.

An **administrative frisk** may be conducted for institutional purposes and within institutional guidelines. Such special-purpose frisks should be for specific and limited purposes. As an example, police at a university may frisk people entering a football stadium for prohibited alcoholic beverages, weapons, horns, etc.

a. Articles taken during a frisk

What may I remove from a person whom I am frisking?

You may remove only those items that you reasonably suspect could be weapons. Examples would be: guns, knives, brass knuckles, nun-chuks, hair picks, screwdrivers and other tools, bottles, chains, etc. If, however, an object you believe to be a weapon is removed, but is not a weapon, yet it is evidence or fruits of a crime, it may be seized. Any item removed pursuant to a valid frisk, or observed in plain view during the frisk, that is evidence of a crime, may be used to support a subsequent arrest or warrant. Remember, you are responsible for any objects taken, and the individual should be told where he or she may recover them later, if they are not illegal to possess.

During an administrative frisk, anything that is the object of the frisk may be taken (e.g., alcoholic beverages).

If, during a frisk, I feel something soft in a pocket, may I remove it?

No. A frisk is a patdown for weapons, only. As an example, while frisking a suspect, you feel something soft, remove it from the person's pocket, and it turns out to be cocaine. If you then arrested the suspect on a narcotics charge, the evidence seized may be suppressed at trial. Under some circumstances, however, the evidence may be used to support a Grand Jury indictment or search warrant. In any event, you may confiscate the cocaine because the individual may not lawfully possess it.

b. Frisking others

If I stop and frisk a person, may I frisk others who are with him or her?

You may frisk them if you believe that they are dangerous to you or others and that they may interfere with your initial stop and its purpose. The mere presence of others at the stop or frisk, however, does not necessarily justify a frisk of them.

c. Frisking the opposite sex

Is it permissible to frisk a suspect of the opposite sex?

From a constitutional perspective, there are no prohibitions about frisking persons of the opposite sex other than those rules which govern the frisking of any suspect. It is important, however, to keep in mind that you should never do anything that a court may consider sufficiently shocking or offensive to social norms, because it could result in your losing the case. Of course, you should abide by any additional guidelines which your agency may have on this issue. Do remember the purpose of frisking and act accordingly.

Normally, because of the opportunity for prior planning and relative proximity of personnel, administrative frisks should be performed by a person of the same sex.

2. Area around suspect

You may extend the frisk to the immediate area around the stopped individual if you feel that he or she is dangerous and may be able to reach a weapon. This extension is solely for the purpose of looking for a weapon. You might, for example, pat down or reach and grab a weapon on the floor of an automobile, or on a blanket if it is in close proximity. The allowable extent of your search is essentially determined by the "jump and reach" rule (see Chapter 7).

3. Examining possessions

If the suspect is in possession of a book satchel, brief case, attaché case, shopping bag, or backpack, may I look in these items for weapons during a frisk?

Except for administrative frisks, generally the answer would be "No" As an example, in a hospital or airport you encounter a suspicious-acting individual carrying a backpack that appears to have a sharp, hard, object inside of it. You could frisk the pack for **weapons**, but you may not search for other items without additional cause. The frisk may, therefore, be extended to a patdown of a bedroll, backpack, etc. The frisk may be used to remove legal weapons (e.g., a knife), if you believe that such a course of action is reasonably necessary for your own protection during the stop. If you remove a legal weapon you must, of course, tell the person where it may be recovered. Of course, in a situation similar to a checkpoint at an airport, a person may be required to submit to a thorough search to proceed further and may also be detained and searched should probable cause arise.

NOTES

CHAPTER 5

ARRESTING A SUSPECT

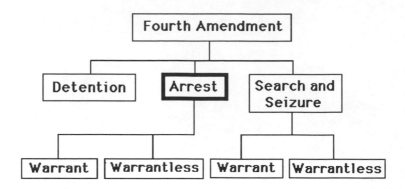

A. BACKGROUND

1. What is an arrest?

You have arrested a person when you have deprived him or her of freedom to come and go by taking him or her into custody. Whether an arrest has been made is determined from the circumstances. The courts routinely say that an arrest has been made if several officers are standing around a person, the officer's weapon is drawn, the person is taken to headquarters, etc. Obviously, a person is under arrest if told so; however, words are not necessary, as actions may indicate the occurrence of an arrest.

A person is not under arrest if he or she volunteers to come to headquarters or to a police station to make a statement and then is free to leave.

May I arrest or restrain an individual who is displaying abnormal or dangerous behavior?

You may take a person into custody for his or her own protection if the person is exhibiting dangerous or abnormal behavior. The individual should be transported immediately to a medical facility and released to appropriate medical personnel. It would be wise to complete a report concerning such an incident. A scenario of this type will not generally be considered an arrest.

Once I have arrested someone, may I release that person myself without the intervention of some judicial authority?

There is no process of unarrest. As a rule an arrested individual should be taken before a magistrate or judge within 48 hours, and any release is within the prerogative of the court. You may release an individual on your own initiative; however, you must be careful of the process because false arrest charges could be raised. Of course, if you have merely stopped a person for investigation, releasing that individual is not a problem.

What is the difference between an arrest and a temporary investigative detention?

A temporary detention for investigation is exactly that — temporary or of short duration. The person is either quickly released or is arrested. During a detention a "Terry" type frisk may be used to look for weapons if you have reason to believe that the suspect may be armed and dangerous.

An arrest involves depriving a person of freedom to come and go, that is, seizing the person. The arrest must be justified if you expect it to continue.

What is the difference between an arrest leading to possible criminal prosecution and an arrest leading to other disciplinary sanctions?

For example, a hospital police officer responding to a fight between two male employees, restrains the apparent aggressor with use of handcuffs, searches him, and removes him to the hospital police office. Feeling that criminal prosecution was not warranted, the officer's intent is to verify the individual's identity, release him as soon as practical, and initiate the hospital's disciplinary procedures.

31

In the above scenario, an administrative seizure is appropriate under such circumstances as a normal arrest (requiring probable cause) and would probably not expose the officer to liability for false arrest.

If during the above search, I find illegal narcotics on the individual, would they be admissible in a criminal prosecution?

The drugs would be admissible because they were removed pursuant to a search incident to an arrest.

Suppose that a university dean tells university police to bring a particular student to the dean's office immediately, but the student refuses to go. May the student be arrested and forcibly brought to the office?

Absent other circumstances, the officer is without authority to seize the student and take him or her into formal custody. If the university regulations provide for such an administrative seizure, then obviously the arrest could be made; however, a conventional arrest is not warranted for administrative purposes. The student could be instructed to appear and may be expelled from campus for failure to do so and, of course, minimal necessary force could be used to accomplish that purpose.

If I issue a citation, is that essentially the same thing as an arrest?

No, not unless you intend it to be and make the arrest pursuant to the probable cause giving rise to the citation or other probable cause. To make an arrest, physical custody must be involved. You may not search incident to a citation.

If I overtly initiate an arrest (such as handcuffing), and during the course of the confrontation I decide that merely writing a citation would suffice, may I write the citation and release the subject?

Yes. However, if you release such an individual, there is an element of liability present for false arrest. This demonstrates the need for being prudent in making an arrest decision.

2. Why arrest?

What are the reasons for arresting a suspect?

In general, you would arrest a person whom you have probable cause to believe has committed a felony, or one who has committed a misdemeanor in your presence, and if you can satisfy any of the three following reasons: (1) to guarantee the person's presence in court, (2) to protect the person or someone else from physical harm, or (3) to prevent the loss or destruction of evidence of the crime. You should NOT arrest a violator "just to teach a lesson."

3. Requirements for an arrest

What are the requirements for a lawful arrest?

You must have the authority, you must be in the appropriate jurisdiction, and you must have a warrant or **probable cause** to believe that a crime was committed and the person you are about to arrest was the perpetrator.

What are the requirements for a lawful administrative arrest?

Because administrative arrests are based on the same general requirements as conventional arrests, they depend on the same foundation. The administrative arrest is different because of the manner in which it will be disposed of, rather than its probable cause foundation.

Do I need a warrant to make an arrest?

In spite of the "warrant requirement" of the Fourth Amendment, you generally do not need a warrant to make a physical arrest for a felony or for a misdemeanor committed in your presence. However, it is a very good idea to obtain a warrant if you have time.

What is the difference between a felony and a misdemeanor?

A **felony** is any offense for which the penalty may exceed more than one year in jail. A **misdemeanor** is any offense for which the penalty is less than one year in jail. A **petit offense** is a type of misdemeanor for which the penalty is further limited.

4. Personal jurisdiction

Personal jurisdiction involves an officer's having physical control (custody) over a subject for the purpose of the judicial process.

Personal jurisdiction of an individual within your jurisdiction may be obtained:

a. pursuant to an arrest
b. pursuant to a warrant
c. by consent or submission
d. by subpoena

Personal jurisdiction outside of your jurisdiction may be obtained:

a. by consent or submission
b. through a federal warrant for unlawful flight to avoid prosecution

34

c. by extradition

If I want to obtain custody of a person who is outside of my jurisdictional boundary (e.g., over the state line), what should I do?

Absent emergency circumstances, the matter should be referred to appropriate local or national authorities.

Suppose that I am outside of my agency's jurisdiction and observe a suspect whom I know is wanted for a felony in my jurisdiction. May I properly arrest that person and return him or her to my jurisdiction?

You may take the suspected felon into custody for the local authorities; then appropriate authorities may take action for extradition. When you take the suspect into custody, you should turn him or her over to local authorities as soon as possible.

How long may I hold an arrestee before I must take him or her before a judge or magistrate?

As a general rule an in-custody suspect must be taken before a magistrate as soon as possible, and in no event later than within forty-eight hours. Some examples of delays even within the forty-eight hours which are unreasonable are delays for the purpose of gathering additional evidence to justify the arrest, a delay motivated by ill will against the arrested individual, or delay for the delay's sake. The government upon demonstration of a *bona fide* emergency may obtain a brief extension, but delays for administrative purposes, hearing consolidations, or intervening weekends do not qualify as extraordinary circumstances. The individual does not bear the burden of proving unreasonable delay; rather the government bears the responsibility of proving a *bona fide* emergency or extraordinary circumstance was present. In general, unnecessary delays may create a risk of false arrest, kidnapping, and the suppression of evidence.

35

B. WARRANT ARRESTS

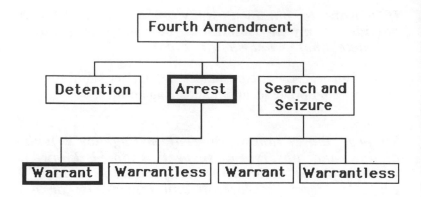

RULE OF LAW: A police officer may arrest any person believed to be named in a valid arrest warrant. This arrest may be pursuant to the knowledge of a warrant even though the warrant is not in hand.

What is an arrest warrant?

An arrest warrant is an order from the issuing court directing an officer or class of officers (e.g., any university police officer) to carry out a particular action, such as take an individual into custody.

What do I need to obtain a warrant for an arrest?

In order to obtain an arrest warrant from a judicial officer (e.g., a judge or magistrate), you will have to demonstrate that you have probable cause for the suspect's arrest for a particular crime. The facts or apparent facts you use to develop your probable cause will have to be presented to the judicial officer in sworn testimony, usually accompanied by a written complaint or affidavit.

If a judge issues an arrest warrant based on the information I provided, am I immune from any liability for an unconstitutional arrest?

Not necessarily. The Court has held that you are granted qualified good-faith immunity only if a reasonable officer would have believed that the facts you presented were adequate to establish probable cause. Thus, a judge's signature on a warrant does not necessarily protect you from liability.

From whom may I obtain an arrest warrant?

Generally arrest warrants may be obtained by appearing before any judge, magistrate, or justice of the peace, regardless of jurisdiction. However, it is advisable to seek an arrest warrant from the judge or magistrate associated with your particular jurisdiction. Federal warrants normally require the judge or magistrate to be of a court of record (i.e., as opposed to a justice of the peace).

When must I have a warrant to make a physical arrest?

Unless it is a true emergency, you must have a warrant to make an arrest under the following conditions:

a.   when you are arresting persons in their own home or in the dwelling of another where they have a right to be,

b.   when you are making an arrest for a misdemeanor not committed in your presence.

What are the restrictions regarding the execution of warrants from other jurisdictions, or in other jurisdictions?

If you are inside your jurisdiction you may:

a.   execute an arrest warrant issued for your jurisdiction for an offense committed in your jurisdiction,

b. hold a person for the proper authorities if you believe your jurisdiction or another jurisdiction issued an arrest warrant for a crime committed elsewhere. You should determine if the warrant is valid on its face (current, etc.).

If you are outside your jurisdiction but within your state you may, depending upon your authority:

a. execute an arrest warrant issued by your jurisdiction for an offense committed in your jurisdiction,

b. assist other officers in the execution of their warrants.

If you are outside your jurisdictional limits and outside your state you may:

a. not execute any arrest warrants unless you are a federal officer,

b. assist other officers in the execution of their warrants.

C. WARRANTLESS ARRESTS

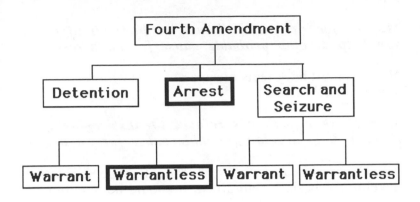

RULE OF LAW: A police officer may arrest, without a warrant, any person committing a misdemeanor in his or her presence or any person whom the officer has probable cause to believe has committed a felony.

Do I have to observe individuals actually committing an offense before I may arrest them for it?

In general, the answer is "No" for felonies and "Yes" for misdemeanors.

If I don't actually observe the felony, what can I use to establish probable cause to arrest the offender?

Any facts or apparent facts which lead you to reasonably believe that the offender probably committed the offense can help develop probable cause. Examples would be: testimonies of others, lying during questioning, furtive activities, difficulty in making a vehicle stop, the presence of burglar tools, a physical description, or the smell of an intoxicating beverage about an individual. When any one fact (or group of facts) makes you believe that (1) a specific crime was probably committed and (2) a given person probably was involved in committing it, then you have probable cause for an arrest.

May a "feeling" or a "hunch" I have about a person help develop probable cause for an arrest?

No. You must have facts or apparent facts with which to develop probable cause.

May I use a person's refusal to answer my questions to help develop probable cause for an arrest?

No. The exercise of a civil right should not be used to help develop the basis for an arrest. It should be remembered, however, that for disciplinary purposes within institutional regulations, you may well have additional authority for inquiry. As an example, the consent or contract relationships may require that persons on the facility (e.g., an airport or hospital) identify themselves when asked by an appropriate authority.

Can an arrest be justified by what I discover after the arrest has been made?

No. You must obtain all the information necessary to establish probable cause for an arrest before it is made. For example, if you arrest a suspect without sufficient probable cause and subsequently discover that he has been selling cocaine on a university campus, that discovery will not validate the arrest.

Under what conditions may I make an arrest for a misdemeanor?

a.   if the arrest is pursuant to a warrant,

b.   if the misdemeanor was committed in your presence,

c.   in some jurisdictions, if you have a witness' signed statement or affidavit,

40

d. under certain conditions in which it is obvious that a suspect committed the misdemeanor, such as finding a drunk behind the steering wheel of a wrecked vehicle. While you did not witness the accident, conditions are sufficiently strong to support an arrest. State statutes vary on this particular issue, and you should be familiar with the laws of your jurisdiction.

Is there a process short of complete arrest through which I can detain an individual pending an inquiry into what appears to be suspicious activity (e.g., the person may not have the right to be within the facility, or is engaging in behaviors contrary to its rules and regulations)?

Yes. Once again, you may employ the administrative stop or arrest as previously noted, because of the unique character of your facility. While frisks for protecting oneself are always permissible, an administrative search may be allowed if you are so empowered by the facility. For example, additional authority is granted at airports for searching for weapons or explosives, or in hospitals for protecting patients from illegal drugs or inappropriate foods or for preservation of the academic atmosphere on a university campus. The right to search incident to an administrative arrest is very limited.

NOTES

CHAPTER 6

SEARCH INCIDENT TO ARREST

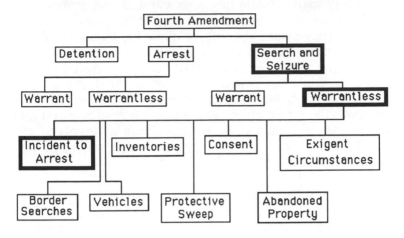

RULE OF LAW: A search may be made pursuant to a valid arrest if the search is contemporaneous in time and place with the arrest. The search includes the person of the individual arrested, the area immediately around the arrestee and items within his or her reach (the "jump and reach" rule).

While specifically allowed incident to arrest, the purpose of the search is to (1) protect the officer or others, (2) prevent the destruction of evidence, and (3) prevent escape or suicide. You should use the warrantless search incident to arrest carefully, because there is no "judicial eye" watching, and evidence you find may be suppressed, whereas it could have been admitted if it were obtained pursuant to a valid warrant. Also, you are prohibited from making a pretextual arrest just to allow a search incident to that arrest.

A. Search of the Individual

If there is a valid arrest, you may properly perform a complete body search, excluding body cavities or a strip search, provided you do so immediately and at the place of the arrest. You may extend the time or move the location only for an urgent need, such as removing the person from a dangerous location where the search will not be interfered with by others. If you have justifiable grounds for doing so, you may remove a person to another area for a strip search. If you made the arrest, either you or persons assisting you may conduct the search. Others not involved, or involved at a later time, may not make the search which was to be performed at the arrest.

This prohibition does not inhibit custodial searches or searches by officers transporting suspects or prisoners. The purpose of such searches, however, is to protect the officer and prevent escape and is limited accordingly. Any evidence found pursuant to such a search may be properly seized.

May I use force to effect an arrest and the ensuing search?

You may use only the amount of force necessary, short of deadly force, to accomplish the arrest and the search incident to that arrest.

Is it permissible to search the opposite sex?

The Constitution does not prohibit your searching a member of the opposite sex. Discretion would suggest, however, that whenever possible another officer who is the same sex as the arrestee should conduct the search. You should, of course, do nothing that would be considered "shocking to the conscience" or social norms, to preclude the possibility of suppression of any evidence found during the search or your being held liable individually. In any case, you should follow your agency's guidelines with respect to searching the opposite sex.

If I arrest suspects with heavy clothing, may I search inside their overcoats, parkas, ski jackets, etc.?

Yes, you may search the individuals regardless of the layers of clothing, and all items within their possession.

B. EXTENT OF SEARCH INCIDENT TO ARREST

Rule of Law: You may search incident to arrest the arrested person and the immediate area around him or her.

What area around the individual am I permitted to search incident to an arrest?

Your search may extend to the area around arrested individuals where they may "jump and reach" a weapon or evidence. As an example, if you arrest a person in an airport lounge, you may search the area around the chair in which the arrestee is seated or the table in front of the suspect before he or she rises. You may look under a nearby table to determine if there is a weapon or the possibility of the destruction of evidence, but this does not include doing a thorough search. Thus, you may not extend the search to other parts or rooms, unless you strongly suspect that others are present who may harm you or others or destroy evidence.

C. SEARCH OF POSSESSIONS

What possessions may I search incident to an arrest?

You may search, incident to an arrest, unsealed items within the possession of the arrestee. You may search handbags, briefcases or similar unlocked items that could hold weapons or evidence. You could also search a suitcase, backpack, book bag, or physician's bag. If you arrest someone in possession of a closed backpack, it may be searched. However, if you take control of the backpack, you would be better off obtaining a warrant before searching it. As an example, near a university stadium you discover two individuals on a blanket who are engaging in the use, sale, or purchase of a half ounce of cocaine. On the blanket is a cooler, a purse, and a backpack. There is also a briefcase which is locked. The individuals' vehicle is parked about 50 feet away from the blanket. Incident to the arrest of the two individuals, you may search their persons, the purse, and the cooler. As for the briefcase, the backpack, and the vehicle, it would be advisable to obtain a warrant to search them.

May I search closed or sealed containers?

If you find any sealed containers in the backpack or cooler, it would be better to obtain a warrant before searching them. Again, you should not search the locked briefcase or the vehicle without first obtaining a search warrant. Because you are responsible for the unprotected property, you should impound the vehicle and perform the necessary *routine* inventory.

Remember, any searches incident to arrest are limited to the time of the arrest, and the privilege vanishes once the arrest is completed and the suspect moved.

D. SEARCH OF VEHICLE INCIDENT TO ARREST

RULE OF LAW: If you arrest an occupant of a vehicle, you may search the interior of the vehicle from which the occupant was removed and any containers therein.

1. **Conventional vehicles**: In addition to searching the interior passenger compartment of the vehicle itself, you may search the trunk or the locked glove compartment if you have reason to believe that they may contain fruits, instrumentalities, or evidence of a crime. It is always wise to obtain a search warrant to search or inspect locked or sealed containers found in the vehicle, unless exigent circumstances war-

rant an immediate search. While there is some support for intrusion into locked or sealed containers without a warrant or exigent circumstances, it is still better to secure such containers and obtain a warrant to open them.

What are exigent circumstances that would allow such a search without a warrant?

For example, you may search a locked suitcase if you believe that it contains dangerous items such as explosives, or that the evidence in the suitcase will be destroyed. You may take possession of any locked or sealed items and hold them pending the issuance of a warrant if you proceed deliberately to obtain the warrant and have reason to believe that they contain evidence of a specific crime.

As another example, if you arrest a person from a vehicle in which there is a closed backpack behind the seat, you may search the backpack, but you should obtain a warrant to search any sealed containers in the backpack. Unsecured or unsealed containers may be opened in the course of a proper search. As a reminder, incident to an administrative search where authority is granted through contract or consent, you may be able to extend the search to all containers without regard to the warrant requirement.

If I arrest a passenger from a vehicle, what is the permissible extent of the vehicle search?

If you arrest a passenger in a vehicle you may search the interior of the vehicle, but not other passengers or their possessions without reasonable cause or exigent circumstances. Similarly, to search the trunk or the locked glove compartment you should have reason to believe that you will find specific evidence relating to the individual arrested.

2. **Recreational vehicles**: Recreational vehicles fall in a unique category of being both vehicle and lodging. The search of the vehicle upon a valid arrest extends to the comparable portion of the RV as it would in a regular vehicle. The passenger compartment (forward area) may be searched,

but the search should not be extended beyond that, without the belief that weapons, evidence or contraband are present and will be destroyed.

The more disabled or stationary the vehicle, the greater the need for a warrant or exigent circumstances. Vehicles, however, may be searched more readily incident to an arrest than other spaces because of their high mobility and their openness to plain view.

What is the permissible extent of a search of a van?

The scope of a search of the interior of a van is similar to that of a conventional vehicle. As a reminder, sealed or locked containers should not normally be searched without a search warrant, exigent circumstances, or strong probable cause.

What is the permissible extent of a search of a motor home?

The interior of a motor home may be searched in a manner similar to that of a conventional vehicle; however, compartments, rooms, and areas closed off from the driving area should not be included in the search incident to arrest without additional probable cause or exigent circumstances. As an example, it would appear that you should not normally search the bathroom incident to an arrest of the driver without exigent circumstances or probable cause requiring such, or unless there is a significant likelihood that the vehicle will be moved.

What is the permissible extent of a search of a slide-in pickup truck camper?

Arrest of an occupant of the pickup does not, in itself, provide a basis for the search of the camper. However, probable cause or exigent circumstances may support the necessity of a search without a warrant.

What is the permissible extent of the search of a recreational vehicle incident to an arrest if the RV is parked?

The more stationary the vehicle, the more it will be treated as a premises and require a search warrant or exigent circumstances. The arrest of an individual in or nearby an RV will allow a search of the individual and the immediate area around the individual, as with any conventional arrest. For example, where a motor home is parked in a hospital or airport parking lot, and the driver is seated in a chair outside of the vehicle, the search would be of the driver and the immediate area around him. If, instead, he were seated inside his RV, the immediate area around him in the vehicle could be searched.

Are unusual vehicles subject to the same rules of search incident to arrest?

You may, incident to arrest, search all varieties of vehicles, including cycles, snowmobiles, all-terrain vehicles, etc.

3. **Aircraft**: The high mobility of aircraft allow them to be treated in the same manner as conventional vehicles. Accordingly, the arrest of the pilot or other occupant will permit a search of the person and the area immediately around him or her. In a small plane this would permit a search of the interior, excluding locked compartments and sealed containers unless exigent circumstances warrant an extension of the search. In a large aircraft you may search in conjunction with the arrest of the pilot the flight deck but you should not extend the search to the aircraft in general without exigent circumstances. As an example, you could search the flight deck, and if you observe what appears to be evidence in the passenger cabin you may seize that evidence under the plain view doctrine. If you have reason to believe that the airplane contains other evidence, fruits, or instrumentalities of a crime, you may detain the aircraft temporarily to obtain a search warrant. The arrest of crew members or passengers

49

would also permit a search of the immediate area around them.

E. INVENTORIES

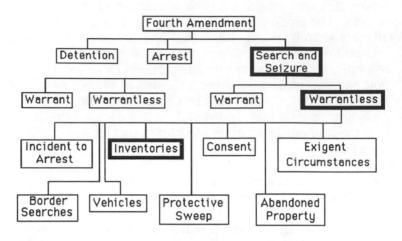

RULE OF LAW: A good-faith routine inventory of personal property is not a search, although evidence, fruits or instrumentalities of a crime discovered incident to the inventory may be seized and properly admitted as evidence. Evidence discovered during the inventory may also be used to support a search warrant. An inventory is NOT a substitute for a search warrant and will be suspect unless it is routine and proper.

You are responsible for property you take or which is left unattended because of an arrest or impoundment removing the operator or owner. Accordingly, you should inventory and secure property left in your control for whatever reason.

What is the extent of an inventory?

Your inventory should be limited to listing in a routine fashion the items you discover. As an example, a sealed envelope should not be opened but listed as a particular item on the inventory. The purpose of an inventory is to protect property and should be carried only as far as necessary for the recording and protection of the property.

May I open containers during my inventory?

Yes, you may open containers in so far as is necessary for identification and accountability of the property. You should not, however, open sealed or locked containers, but mark them for identification.

What are some examples of items that could be opened during an inventory?

You may open any unsealed containers such as: camera cases, pocketbooks, coolers, open envelopes, tobacco cans, film canisters, briefcases, picnic baskets, beach bags, etc.

You may also open the hood or trunk of a vehicle, or remove the hubcaps and battery and place them in the trunk for safe keeping. However, you should not cause damage to the vehicle (e.g., cut open the seats or door panels).

May I inventory impounded vehicles at random?

No. You should follow a routine inventory procedure. Your department should establish clear written guidelines setting forth the inventory procedures. For example, you should have a routine inventory checklist for vehicles to be used for every impounded, confiscated, or held vehicle.

Is there a difference between inventorying vehicles and other property?

No. The guidelines are essentially the same, and you should follow a routine procedure for inventorying any property that comes into your possession. For example, you could inventory the contents of an arrested individual's suitcase, provided that you do not break any sealed containers. You may, however, seize any evidence, fruits or instrumentalities of a crime discovered in the course of a proper inventory.

Should my agency have a written inventory procedure?

Yes. The Court has consistently reaffirmed the importance of a written inventory policy that is strictly followed. An example of a model inventory policy is provided as a guide in chapter 14 of this book.

What if, during an inventory, I find evidence of a crime?

To insure that any further evidence is admissible, it would be wise to stop the inventory immediately, secure the property, and seek a search warrant for the vehicle/property.

F. SEARCH INCIDENT TO A CITATION

Do I have the authority to search an individual incident to writing him or her a citation?

No. You may **NOT** search the person of an individual to whom you have issued a citation or court summons, if you do not plan to take that person into physical custody. However, if you believe the individual to be armed and dangerous, you may frisk him or her for weapons.

Do I have the authority to search the area around a visitor to whom I have written a citation?

No. The issuance of a citation or summons does NOT as a rule justify a search of the area around the person being issued the citation or summons. For example, if you observe a person smoking marijuana in a vehicle in a parking lot, and you confiscate the cigarette and issue a citation, you are not justified in searching the vehicle, hoping to find a "baggie" of marijuana. However, state law and agency regulations may vary on this issue, and you are encouraged to become familiar with the particular guidelines under which you must operate.

NOTES

CHAPTER 7

SEARCH AND SEIZURE

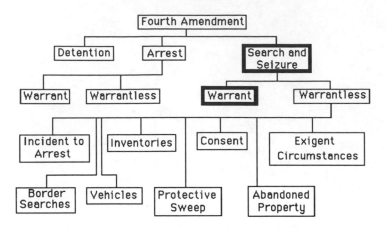

A. Searches with a Warrant

If you have probable cause to believe that contraband or evidence of a crime is in a particular location, you may present under oath or affirmation the facts or apparent facts before a judge or magistrate and request that a search warrant be issued. In order to obtain a search warrant, you will also have to specify (1) the object or objects to be seized and (2) the particular location where the object(s) are to be found.

Because of the "warrant requirement" of the Fourth Amendment, it is generally good policy to obtain a warrant before searching anyone's private property. Failure to obtain a warrant prior to a search may result in the inadmissibility of that evidence in court, and could expose you to liability. Currently, the courts appear to be moving in the direction of increased reliance on search warrants.

What is a search warrant?

A warrant is an order from the issuing court directing an officer or class of officers (e.g., any state university police officer) to carry out a particular action, such as conduct a search for illegal drugs or related paraphernalia.

From whom may I obtain a search warrant?

Like arrest warrants, search warrants may be obtained by appearing before any judge, magistrate, or justice of the peace, regardless of jurisdiction. However, it is advisable to seek an arrest warrant from the judge or magistrate associated with your particular jurisdiction. Federal warrants normally require the judge or magistrate to be of a court of record (i.e., as opposed to a justice of the peace).

What kinds of information may I use to establish probable cause for a search warrant?

You may use personal knowledge or observation, or information obtained from a reliable source that you believe to be accurate. The accuracy may be determined by your observation of events following the report of the informant. For example, a student on a university campus approaches you and tells you that a student appears to be selling drugs from a late model van. You observe the student handing a small package to another person. You may seek a search warrant for the vehicle, based on your informant's report and your observation.

May I obtain a search warrant by providing a judge with the necessary information over the telephone?

Although some jurisdictions may apply other restrictions, case and statutory law today generally allows telephonic warrants for circumstances in which it is impossible or impractical for you to physically appear before a judge or magistrate first. Of course, such warrant applications must eventually be supported by the same evidence or affidavit as any other warrant. The telephonic warrant should be used for urgent situations, not merely inconvenient ones.

What are the restrictions on a search with a warrant?

There are seven basic restrictions:

a. A member of the class of officers, although he or she may be assisted by other officers, to whom the warrant is directed must be present at the search and should generally be the first to initiate execution (entry, etc.). As an example, a warrant directed to an airport police officer to search a tenant's building for drugs or evidence thereof should be carried out by at least one airport police officer, but he or she may be assisted by others, for example city police, sheriff deputies, drug agents, etc.

b. The search warrant must be executed within a reasonable time period after its issuance. As a general rule, a week should be an adequate time to complete the execution of the warrant. Local rules will dictate the time of return of the warrant. If your warrant is not executed in a timely manner, a new warrant may be necessary. It is not uncommon for new evidence to be required to obtain a new warrant to replace a warrant not executed in a timely manner.

c. The search must take place in the particular location directed by the warrant. For example, a warrant to search for stolen university equipment in a house may be extended to those buildings at the address or location specified in the warrant that are in close proximity to the house. A warrant to search the garage for a stolen tractor, however, would not extend to other buildings, including the house.

d. The search must be for the particular item(s) specified in the warrant, and you may search only in places where the item(s) could reasonably be located. If you have a warrant for narcotics, you could look in all places where narcotics may be hidden, such as a refrigerator, medicine cabinet, closet, or drawers. If, on the other hand, you are searching for a stolen television set, you could search

56

only where a television set could be, such as a cabinet. You could not, of course, search for an elephant in a medicine cabinet. See "Elephant Rule" in the glossary.

e. The warrant, with the list of items seized and all appropriate inventories, must be returned to the court, within the prescribed, or a reasonable, time. If the warrant is not returned in a timely manner the officer must be prepared to explain the delay and face possible loss of the evidence.

f. A warrant issued is normally valid for the daytime unless night searches are specified or the statutory laws of the jurisdiction permit nighttime searches. A warrant for the daytime may, however, be started in the day and continued into the night if done in a consistent and deliberate manner and if it is not done for harassment.

g. A search warrant is valid only for a single search expedition. If the need arises for a return to the premises a new warrant should be obtained.

If I am executing a search warrant for stolen signs, and I find narcotics in a medicine cabinet and a stolen chain saw in the garage, may I seize them and use them as evidence?

You may use the stolen chain saw as evidence because it was found in a location where signs could be hidden. The narcotics, on the other hand, should be inadmissible because they were found in a location outside of the scope of the warrant. See "Elephant Rule."

While conducting a premises search pursuant to a search warrant, may I search any individuals present?

You may always perform a "Terry" frisk if you have reason to believe that the individuals are armed and dangerous, and you may prevent any individuals from interfering with the search. However, you may search these individuals only on the basis of probable cause that they have in their possession objects that are the target of the search or, based on circumstances present, that they have on their person evidence or contraband of a particular crime.

What are the jurisdictional restrictions on executing search warrants?

If you are within your jurisdiction, you may:

a. execute a search warrant issued for your jurisdiction and related to criminal activity in your jurisdiction.

If you are outside your jurisdiction, depending on your statutory authority, but within your state you may:

a. execute a search warrant issued for your jurisdiction and for criminal conduct related to your scope of activity,

b. assist other officers in the execution of their search warrants.

If you are outside your jurisdiction and outside your state you may:

a. not execute any search warrants unless you are a federal officer,

b. assist other officers in the execution of their warrants.

Although your authority may allow you to serve warrants in some of the above situations, as a general rule, it would be wise to refer the matter to the appropriate local authorities for action.

B. SEARCHES WITHOUT A WARRANT

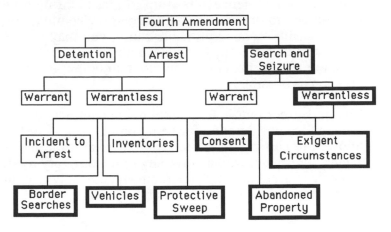

*Are there any exceptions to the warrant require-
ment for a search?*

Yes. Legal tradition has created eight exceptions to the warrant requirement for a search:

1. **Searches incident to arrest**: These searches were
discussed in Chapter 6 of this book. They are limited in
scope, and in general they would not include locked or
sealed containers.

2. **Inventories**: The purpose of an inventory is to secure
property left in your control for whatever reason. Inventories
were also discussed in Chapter 6 of this book.

3. **Consent searches**: These searches are generally difficult to uphold in court unless you obtain a valid consent, and
they should be used only as a last resort. In order for the
consent to be valid, it must be made in the absence of duress
or intimidation, a condition not typical of most people under
arrest. It is a good idea to inform an individual from whom
you want consent for a search that he or she is free to deny
consent. Once consent is given, the party is free to ask the
officers to discontinue the search at any time.

59

If you are asked to stop the consent search, you should do so. However, all evidence seized up to that point may be used in court or to obtain a search warrant for continuation of the search. If you have probable cause, you may secure the premises, vehicle, or possessions to obtain a warrant and continue the search, provided you move to obtain the warrant as soon as possible.

As a reminder, consent is frequently given contractually or by privilege in consideration for being on the facility or being allowed to participate in the activity. As an example, a contractual agreement with a university for a dormitory room may include consent to search the room and the individual in it. It may even include consent to search a vehicle parked on the campus.

What about special consent situations, i.e., prior to entering a football stadium or commercial airplane?

In such situations where consent exists, the search authority will permit a search only to the extent warranted by the circumstances. As an example, a person attempting to enter a stadium might be searched for alcoholic beverages or dangerous instrumentalities or, in an airport, for weapons or explosives. The search is based entirely on consent and the person must submit or may be refused access.

Who may legitimately consent to a search?

In order for persons to give consent to a search, they must appear to have a legitimate control over the area or things to be searched. For example, consider the following situations:

a. The owner or operator of a motor home could consent to having it searched for drugs that his son may be selling.

b. A person carrying a briefcase through an airport could generally consent to having it searched.

c.   The manager of an airport hotel could consent to the search of a guest's room if it is past checkout time, and the guest had not paid for the following evening, unless standard procedures were simply to allow the guest to stay over and settle the bill at the end. If later settlement is allowed then in order for the consent search to be justified, the abandonment must be apparent, such as the guest not being in the room for a day or two, removing all the luggage, loading it, driving away, etc. The abandonment of the premises should be evident, either actual or apparent. A brief time after the checkout time may not be abandonment but a substantial time, several hours or actual departure, probably would be.

d.   The manager of the airport hotel could **not** consent to the search of a guest's room in which the guest was legitimately registered.

e.   A resident or roommate in a university dorm could **not** consent to a search of her roommate's personal belongings. The roommate could, however, consent to a search of the jointly-occupied premises, and plain view discoveries may lead to a search of the personal belongings of the roommate. A search warrant is, of course, better to preserve the use of evidence. As an example, a warrant may be obtained on the basis of plain-view discovery so that the subsequent search is protected. The premises could be secured for a reasonable time (overnight) to prevent the removal or destruction of evidence.

g.   The manager of fitness facilities could **not** normally consent to a search of a locker legitimately rented by a third party, until it is abandoned or the leased time has lapsed.

h.   A student could **not** consent to the search of his or her friend's backpack, book bag, or briefcase.

Does consent to search a vehicle extend to closed containers found inside the vehicle?

It is reasonable to consider the suspect's consent to include examination of unlocked, unsealed containers that may reasonably contain the object of the search. There must be specific consent for the search of any sealed or locked containers, and a suspect may limit the scope of the search at any time.

4. **Exigent (emergency) circumstances**: If it is a true emergency and you are unable to take the time to obtain a search warrant, you may conduct a warrantless search. For example, you may hear screams coming from inside an airport motel room or university dormitory room. You may see what appears to be blood dripping from the trunk of a car, or you may have reason to believe that a bomb has been placed in some location that is privately controlled. You may believe that if you take time to obtain a warrant, the evidence will be destroyed or removed, or you may believe that someone's life may be in danger.

Because of your special institutional role your authority will normally be expanded as you will undoubtedly find in your guidelines. You may have exigent circumstances to preserve the institutional purpose, prevent access to illegal or dangerous objects, and remove dangerous or prohibited items or personnel.

5. **The vehicle exception**:

a. **Automobiles**: The openness and mobility of vehicles allow you to search them more readily than other areas. As a general rule, vehicle searches may be conducted if you have reason to believe that the vehicle contains specific evidence of a crime and that a delay in obtaining a warrant will result in the loss of the evidence. You may, of course, secure the vehicle and proceed immediately to obtain a warrant. You may use plain-view observation of the interior and exterior to support a warrant. As an example, you observe what you believe to be a "baggie" of marijuana on the floor of the van. You could secure the vehicle and seek a warrant, or if you believe that it will be moved and the evidence destroyed you may proceed to seize the evidence.

The difficulty in searching a vehicle not incident to arrest and without a warrant is that you run the risk of being unable to persuade the court that your action was the only alternative and that the need was sufficient to proceed without a warrant.

b. **Aircraft**: Aircraft should be treated in the same manner as boats and conventional vehicles. As with boats, airplanes may be boarded for safety inspections, and evidence observed in plain view may be seized and used to support an arrest or warrant.

An aircraft may be boarded without a warrant if there are exigent circumstances or probable cause that it contains evidence of a crime or violations of hunting or fishing limits.

6. **Protective sweeps**: Where there is a legitimate need to secure an area for such purposes as: public safety (e.g., bomb threat), dignitary protection, protection of officers conducting searches, prevention of the destruction of evidence, etc., you may perform a protective sweep of the area. Evidence discovered during the course of a proper sweep can be seized.

7. **Abandoned property**: Property that has been discarded may be searched without a warrant. This would include such things as: any property that is discarded by a suspect attempting to avoid discovery by law enforcement officers, thrown out the window of a vehicle or a room, left unattended in a public area for an extended period of time, remaining in a hotel room, dormitory room, or storage room after a person has checked out, etc.

Additionally, garbage placed for collection or discard at the point where the public or animals would have access to it is generally considered abandoned. For example, items in a garbage container by a dormitory room or in a parking lot could be searched without a warrant.

8. Border (international boundary) searches: Individuals attempting to enter the United States at the border or when they land at airports are subject to a complete search of their person and all property in their possession.

NOTES

CHAPTER 8

SUSPECT IDENTIFICATION

RULE OF LAW: A witness identification of a suspect will generally be admissible in court so long as the identification procedure is not unduly suggestive.

Suspect identification by a witness may be accomplished by single identification, photographic identification, and lineup identification. In each of the situations care must be taken to avoid unnecessary suggestibility as to a particular accused. Timeliness is also an important factor.

A. SINGLE IDENTIFICATION

Single identification occurs when you apprehend a suspect shortly after and in the vicinity of a crime and return that suspect to the victim/witness for identification. The logic of the court is that you are as likely to free the innocent as identify the guilty. The procedure should be accomplished with the least possible delay, and there should be no suggestion or influence by the officer.

How much delay is permissible in a single identification?

The time should be measured in minutes and not hours. As an example, an airport employee reports seeing someone break into a vehicle in a parking lot. Twenty minutes later you apprehend a person matching the description. You may take that person back to the employee for identification. If, however, the person is apprehended several hours later, such an identification would be inappropriate; rather, identification should be made through a photographic or physical lineup.

What if the suspect insists on an immediate identification?

Regardless of the time frame, if an apprehended suspect insists on being returned for immediate identification by a victim/witness, you may conduct such an identification or hold the suspect for a conventional lineup as soon as possible.

Suppose the identification cannot be made until later because the witness is being treated in a hospital. May a single identification still be made?

Yes. Because you are as likely to free the innocent as identify the guilty, you may use the bedside identification if such proves necessary because of the witness' condition or other exigent circumstances. A photographic identification may also be employed under these circumstances.

May the witness be asked if this is the person who committed the offense?

Yes. You may ask, "Is this the person who committed the offense?" You would be wise to precede the question with the statement that all persons closely matching the description are being brought in for identification.

B. PHOTOGRAPHIC LINEUPS

Under conditions when a physical lineup is not feasible or appropriate, a witness may be asked to identify a suspect from a group of photographs. As with any general lineup procedure, the pictures should not be presented in any suggestive manner, sequence, or pattern. Furthermore, the photographs of the non-suspects should match the general appearance of the suspect.

How many pictures should be in a photographic lineup?

Obviously, the more pictures of different individuals shown to the witness, the more likely the identification will be free from taint. As an example, a photographic lineup that includes the suspect and three or four pictures of other individuals would be sufficient. The aim is to require the witness to independently undergo a non-suggestive decision-making process.

Can a single picture be used in a photographic lineup?

Yes. A single picture may be used under some circumstances, such as following an armed robbery where the suspect is known, the modus operandi (M.O.), is similar, and the suspect is armed and dangerous. The application of rules of exigency are wise here, and you are always better off using more than one photograph to avoid the taint of suggestibility.

C. Conventional Lineups

A conventional lineup is one conducted of several individuals, one of whom is the suspect. The lineup should always include individuals of the same race and sex and of similar build and characteristics. For example, a suspect of medium build and height, with a beard, should be placed in a lineup with other persons also of a similar build, with a beard, and all with close hair color.

If my suspect is six feet tall, must all of the persons in the lineup be six feet tall?

The suspect must not stand out as the only person six feet tall, if such is a factor, but you may have others of similar size, give or take approximately two inches.

If my suspect has dark skin, must all others be of the same tone?

The tone should be as close as possible but does not have to match exactly. As an example, a light skinned person of a dark race may be included with a tanned person if other characteristics are satisfactory.

What should I do if I can find only one other person of similar description?

This would be an ideal time to use a photographic lineup of the suspect and others, using mug shots. If the time frame is short enough a single identification may be appropriate. Otherwise, forego the lineup at this stage and secure a good written description. Do take a photograph of the suspect to be placed with others at a later time. If the matter is of sufficient importance, remember that the witness can be held or delayed a reasonable time. The witness could become hostile, however, so you must use discretion in such situations.

How many persons other than the suspect need I have in a lineup?

Obviously the more the better, but three or four more than the suspect is probably adequate.

Does a suspect have a right to have his or her lawyer present during a physical lineup?

Yes. Unlike the single identification and the photographic lineup, a suspect has a right to have a lawyer present during a physical lineup, if the individual has been formally charged. It is wise to provide the opportunity for counsel if the person is the principle suspect.

NOTES

CHAPTER 9
EVIDENCE

A. DEFINITION

Evidence is any form of proof, or probative matter, legally presented at a trial by the parties through the use of witnesses, records, documents, and concrete objects for the purpose of inducing belief in the minds of the court or jury. Evidence includes the presentation of any facts in a case that tend to either confirm or deny the truth of an assertion made by one of the parties in the case.

Evidence could also be of value for administrative hearings (e.g., disciplinary or termination hearings). When used for this purpose, the standards of evidence are generally not the same for administrative hearings as for judicial hearings.

What types of evidence are there?

Evidence may be either *direct* or *circumstantial.*

Direct evidence is any evidence that, in and of itself, tends to confirm an element or issue in question in the trial, without the need to produce other facts necessary to its introduction. An example would be eye witness testimony.

Circumstantial evidence is indirect evidence; that is, it involves facts from which the truth of an issue may be logically inferred. An example would be fingerprints on the murder weapon or testimony from a witness that he was in the area at the time the shot was heard and saw the defendant near the scene at about the time of the offense.

What are the different categories of evidence?

Evidence may be **testimonial**; that is, provided in the form of a testimony by a person, such as an eye witness or a person giving a confession.

71

Evidence may be **documentary**; that is, every form of writing, such as the guest register of the airport inn or a concessioner's financial records.

Evidence may be **real**; that is, all items directly involved in the incident such as blood stains, tire marks, powder burns, or a gun.

Demonstrative evidence is normally relevant and admissible if it demonstrates that the crime was committed and sheds some light on how it was committed. It includes weapons, blood-stained clothing, lifted fingerprints, photographs, mock-ups, models and similar items to aid in understanding the testimony.

Normally the conclusions or opinions of a witness are irrelevant and accordingly inadmissible. Qualified witnesses may render estimates or opinions of sobriety, age, race, speed, etc. Experts may testify and give professional opinions only in the area of their expertise, but they may not testify about common matters.

B. ADMISSIBILITY OF EVIDENCE

What is required to get evidence admitted at trial?

1. The evidence must be **relevant**; it must have some bearing on the facts at issue in the case. The question to ask is, does the evidence tend to prove or disprove the guilt of a person charged with a crime? As an example, evidence showing that a defendant owned a large mixed ring of General Motors keys might be relevant if the accused is charged with illegally entering General Motors vehicles on a university campus and taking property from them.

2. The evidence must be **trustworthy**; it must be demonstrated that the evidence was not altered or tampered with. The *chain of custody* is an important means of preserving the integrity of the evidence as it is transferred from one person to another.

3. The evidence must be **competent**; that is, it must have been obtained within the constitutional guidelines (most often the Fourth and Fifth Amendments), or it may be subject to suppression under the *Exclusionary Rule.*

Under what conditions may I legally obtain physical or documentary evidence of a crime?

a. If you observe it in plain view when you had a legitimate right to be where you were when you saw it,

b. if you have a valid warrant to search for it,

c. if you have a valid consent to search for it,

d. if you discover it during a search incident to a valid arrest,

e. if someone willingly gives it to you,

f. if you discover it on public or in abandoned property,

g. if you find abandoned property that itself becomes evidence,

h. if you discover it during a valid inventory of a vehicle or other item,

i. if you inadvertently discover it during the course of a proper "Terry" frisk.

C. Chain of Custody

How do I protect the chain of custody?

To demonstrate the trustworthiness of any evidence you must be able to do the following two things:

1. account for and document its whereabouts from the time you discovered it until it is entered at trial.

73

2. detail who had access to it from the time you discovered it until it is entered at trial.

For example, you seize a pound of marijuana that you discover in a vehicle you were searching incident to the arrest of its driver for selling drugs in a hospital parking lot. You place the evidence in a sealed container and tag it with information regarding when, where, and from whom it was seized and who seized it. You then turn the evidence over to someone who is in charge of the locked property room, safe, or other system for storing evidence in a secure manner. Furthermore, you document the transfer on paper.

Similarly, any time the evidence is moved or changes hands it should be documented in writing, until it is finally admitted at trial. At no point in its "chain" should there be a possibility of tampering with or altering the evidence.

What if I intend to send evidence through the mail?

Any evidence sent through the mail should be sent "registered" which means that it travels in a secured way and must be signed for upon delivery. For example, you arrest a person for driving while intoxicated on port authority property. The person submits to a blood alcohol test at the local hospital. At the hospital you witness the drawing of the sample, seal the container and mail it to a forensic laboratory for analysis. The package should be sent by "registered" mail. Unless the laboratory is familiar with procedures for handling evidence, you should request that it be returned by registered mail.

D. RULES OF EVIDENCE

What are the Rules of Evidence?

Both the federal and state court systems have written rules or guidelines that establish the admissibility of evidence at trial. These rules are actually rules of process or exclusion; they elaborate what will be acceptable and unacceptable as evidence, and how the evidence should be offered.

What are some examples of rules of evidence?

1. **Best Evidence Rule**: This rule requires that the most reliable proof of a fact be utilized. As an example, the original written document is best evidence, not a copy or photocopy. Thus, the airport motel's guest register is admitted to show that a particular person signed it, whereas a photocopy would be admitted only if the original register were lost, destroyed, or completely unusable or is unavailable.

2. **Hearsay Rule**: Hearsay evidence is what a witness heard another person say and is generally inadmissible to prove the truth of a fact at issue. It may be admissible under some circumstances, such as a dying declaration, or an admission against interest of the declarant. As an example, one university student testifies that another student said that he had bought narcotics from the parking garage attendant. This would be inadmissible as hearsay; however, it might be used to support a warrant. If, on the other hand, one student testified that she used narcotics with another student who said he bought them from the attendant, it is probably admissible because it represents a statement against her own interest.

Remember that hearsay may be acceptable at administrative hearings.

E. ADMISSIONS AND CONFESSIONS

An **admission** is normally less than a confession, but it is a statement against personal interest. Guilt may be inferred from an admission that acknowledges facts which, when combined with other facts, will produce such a conclusion.

A **confession** is the total acknowledgement of the accused that he or she is guilty of the offense charged.

F. THE EXCLUSIONARY RULE

The **exclusionary rule** is an artificial rule created by the courts that allows the court or defendant to suppress valid evidence for trial purposes if it was illegally obtained by officers or agents of the government acting under color of law. The evidence may be admissible for other purposes, such as Grand Jury evidence, preliminary hearings, impeachment of witnesses not telling the truth on the stand in the trial, etc.

Normally a motion to suppress evidence will be heard at a pre-trial hearing and, in some instances, in the trial process itself. The officer obtaining the evidence will normally be called to support its use, and any other persons will be heard to support or deny its use. The judge will make the decision to suppress or admit the evidence, and he or she may do so at the hearing, shortly after it, or take the matter under advisement for a ruling at a later time. It is also possible that the "taint" may be purged by eventual discovery or some other curative action.

As a rule, the Exclusionary Rule does not apply to administrative matters.

What does it mean to "purge the taint"?

Although evidence may be suppressible because of the way it was collected (seized), the "taint" created by the officer's action might be cured by other existing circumstances. As an example, eventual discovery, standing, or the existence of other relevant evidence may permit the use of the evidence in some form. In other words, if the use of evidence is blocked because of some constitutional violation, there is a possibility that it might be admitted through some other avenue.

What is standing?

Standing refers to the right of a person to contest the admissibility of evidence because his or her individual constitutional rights were violated. As an example, you have no right (standing) to complain about a constitutional violation if you are not an injured party. Standing is frequently determined by possession or ownership.

Should I destroy or release evidence that was seized under questionable circumstances?

No. Because of the possibility of purging the taint, the evidence may not be suppressed by the court, and even if it is it may be valuable at trial to impeach a witness not telling the truth. The evidence may also be used in grand jury hearings and preliminary hearings unless prohibited by law. Additionally, it may be of value in administrative hearings.

Should I try to make evidence that I have obtained conform to the desires of the court in order to preserve it?

Not as stated, but you should make your actions and procedures conform to good constitutional standards so that you have protected evidence and can rely on good faith in your actions. You should, of course, protect evidence so that the chain of custody is followed and the evidence is preserved.

To what does the fruit of the "poisonous tree" refer?

Otherwise legal and proper evidence obtained as the product of other illegal police activity may not, as a rule, be admitted at trial. You should always check with the prosecutor's office if you have questions regarding the propriety of any evidence in your possession.

NOTES

CHAPTER 10

TALKING WITH SUSPECTS

A. CONVENTIONAL CONVERSATION

Because of their unique role, it would not be considered inappropriate for police, for example, to casually approach some people on a sidewalk or in a corridor and make "small talk" with them. Nor would it be inappropriate after dark to approach an individual and ask if everything is alright. Such intrusions would not generally be considered unreasonable as long as they do not interfere with the individual's activities and are not intruding unnecessarily into his or her privacy. Furthermore, in many public facilities, the police officer may (probably has an absolute right to) request identification and inquire into the purpose of a person's presence.

Of course, this latitude given to you as an institutional police officer works to your advantage when you are suspicious that criminal activity may be present. Because you may make such contacts legitimately, anything you may observe, hear, or smell of an illegal nature during such a contact would serve to help develop probable cause for further legal action. For example, you approach a parked car in the parking lot at 3:00 A.M. to inquire whether the occupants are in need of assistance, and you see a "baggie" of what appears to be marijuana in plain view in the ashtray. You could confiscate the baggie and write a citation or make an arrest for the controlled substance.

Again, while individuals may be under no obligation to talk to you, they may be required to produce identification and a satisfactory reason why they are at a particular location, or be subject to expulsion or arrest. Good faith on your part is an important factor.

B. ADMINISTRATIVE CONTACTS

In order to conduct agency administrative tasks, police have the right to initiate contacts with people when appropriate. Examples of such contacts would include: checks for parking permits, authorizations to be in certain areas of the facility, possession of plane tickets, etc. If, during such a contact, you detect illegal activity, you could pursue it further. For example, you approach a person on a college campus at night to ascertain if she possesses a valid student identification and, upon contacting her, notice that she is carrying a burning hash pipe. Your discovery would provide a legal basis for a citation or arrest. Or, you contact a person studying in a classroom late at night, and you observe that he is in possession of a backpack with unique markings that matches the description of one that had been stolen in the library earlier that day. You may seize the backpack and arrest the person.

As in the case of conventional conversation, people are under no legal obligation to answer your questions in these administrative situations. Their failure to do so, however, may mean that they are violating some law, rule or regulation that would allow you to take further action. For example, a campus police officer approaches a person at night and asks to see her student identification, but she refuses to produce one. Such an action on her part could, of course, lead to a citation or arrest for trespass.

C. INVESTIGATIVE CONTACTS

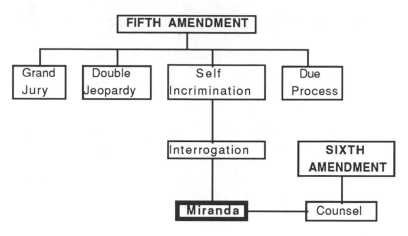

If you have reason to believe that a crime may have occurred and you are investigating the incident further, you have a right to ask questions of people whom you reasonably feel may have some knowledge of the incident. These people fall into two categories: (a) those who may have some information about the incident but are not suspects, and (b) those who may have some knowledge about the incident because they are suspects or potential suspects.

Furthermore, in this second group there are two subcategories: (1) those whom you have no intention of taking into physical custody and (2) those whom you may take into custody. It is important to remember that, for prosecutorial purposes, **no one** in any of the above categories is under any legal obligation to tell you **anything**.

If you plan to question a suspect, it is always wise to provide him or her with the "Miranda" warnings. It is **necessary** to provide the suspect with "Miranda" warnings if you take him or her into custody and are going to interrogate that person.

What rights are included in the Miranda warnings?

The suspect must be advised of the following:

a. You have a right to remain silent.

b. Anything you say can be used against you in a court of law.

c. You have a right to have a lawyer, either of your own choice or court appointed, if you cannot afford one.

d. You have a right to talk to your lawyer before answering any questions and to have him or her present during any questioning, if you wish.

When must I read the Miranda rights to a suspect?

While actually reading the Miranda warnings may be best for accuracy or procedure, you may just state them if you are confident that you can repeat the content accurately. Miranda warnings must be provided before questioning anyone whom you intend to take into physical custody (i.e., arrest). Also, it is an excellent idea to inform people of their Miranda rights in the following circumstances:

a. if you ask a person to accompany you to headquarters or to the headquarters or to another police department for questioning,

b. before you question a person whom you have placed in your patrol car,

c. before you question a suspect to whom the Miranda warnings have not been read for several hours; or if you are unaware that they have been given recently,

d. before you question a suspect after someone else has read him or her the Miranda warnings during a prior questioning,

e. if you had to use physical force to gain a person's compliance for a frisk, arrest, or search.

After waiving Miranda rights and answering some questions, may a suspect refuse to answer any further questions?

Yes. If a suspect waives Miranda rights and agrees to answer your questions, he or she still has the right to stop answering questions at any point during the interrogation.

It is important to remember that in any subsequent proceedings it will be your responsibility to prove waiver.

After waiving his Miranda rights, a suspect decides to talk to me. If his or her attorney is waiting to speak to him or her, do I have to inform the suspect?

No. Although it may be a better procedure to so inform the suspect, it is not necessary. The privilege of asking for the advice of an attorney accrues to the suspect and not the attorney.

Before informing a suspect of his or her Miranda rights, do I have to disclose the subject matter of the intended interrogation?

No. The important thing is to insure that the suspect is aware of his or her rights so he or she may request assistance of counsel or elect to remain silent.

May I reinitiate interrogation without counsel present after the suspect has requested and been provided counsel?

No. You may not reinitiate interrogation without counsel present after the accused has requested and been provided counsel. The Fifth Amendment protection is not terminated or suspended after the suspect has consulted with an attorney. Before reinitiating interrogation, you should consult with the suspect's counsel.

As a reminder — you are the one who will have to convince the court that you have provided the warnings by your actions, procedures, obvious good faith actions, etc.

D. TALKING WITH FOREIGN NATIONALS

If you have a law enforcement encounter with a foreign national with whom you have difficulty communicating, you should obtain a translator or forego questioning. Notify your supervisor and the nearest appropriate prosecutor's office if you take the individual into custody.

E. TALKING WITH PERSONS WITH SPEECH OR HEARING PROBLEMS

If you have a law enforcement encounter with a person with speech or hearing difficulties, you should obtain a person who can sign or respond appropriately. If you cannot do so, forego questioning. If you effect an arrest, notify your supervisor, the nearest office that can provide assistance to the handicapped person, and the nearest appropriate prosecutor's office.

NOTES

CHAPTER 11

SURVEILLANCE

A. SURVEILLANCE BY OFFICERS

You may observe anything from a place you have a right to be. You may use any device to aid your visual surveillance such as binoculars, a telescope, infrared devices, etc. You should not use observable devices such as a flashlight because the observation process should not obviously intrude into privacy. The key to proper surveillance is to remember that the target has a **reasonable expectation of privacy** and you may intrude only when you have a real need for the information. If electronic surveillance is utilized, you should be prepared to show that this is the only way or only safe way the information can be obtained.

Surveillance may be conducted from another vehicle, from a roof, an aircraft, a boat, an adjoining building, etc. Anything you observe during your surveillance may be used as evidence or to support an arrest or search warrant.

What is a curtilage?

A **curtilage** is a dwelling and the immediate area around it in which there is a reasonable expectation of privacy acceptable to society. A dwelling is a place where people reside and has been set aside for their exclusive use. Dwellings include: homes, condominiums, apartments, rented rooms, cabins, mobile home sites, and any out buildings within a reasonable proximity that have been set aside for that exclusive use.

What is the extent of a curtilage?

The curtilage includes the special area of family privacy within the "picket fence." It does not include buildings some distance from the home, areas across a public road, or places of business.

What are the relevant rules regarding surveillance with respect to a curtilage?

You have a right to engage in surveillance of a curtilage so long as you are not on the curtilage and do not intrude onto it. As an example, you may observe from the public road, from an open field, from outside the fence, from an adjacent building, or from an aircraft. You may not encroach by physical intrusion onto the curtilage itself. Specifically, as part of a drug investigation, you should not sneak up to a married student's apartment and peer in the window looking for signs of drug trafficking.

May I approach and peer in the window of a motor home that is parked in the hospital parking lot?

Yes, you may, especially if it appears as though it is illegally parked there over night. In this situation the reasonable expectation of privacy is reduced.

May I use binoculars, night scopes or bionic ears to observe activity within a curtilage as long as I don't physically intrude onto it?

Yes, you may use binoculars or night scopes. However, if your surveillance is to involve electronic listening devices, you should obtain the necessary warrant because of the planned nature of the intrusion. Plain hearing or listening does not require a warrant and may be used as evidence or to support an arrest or a warrant.

The courts seem to be moving toward allowing the enhancement of vision from your own non-intrusive position. Heat sensors and light enhancement devices would seem to be permissible. Sound enhancement, however, must not fall into the electronic eavesdropping category (for which you need a warrant).

May I set up a vehicle from which to observe activity in an adjoining vehicle?

Yes. You may observe all activity you can see (including use of binoculars or scopes) and use the observation to support a warrant or effect an arrest. You may use a recording device (e.g., recording from the vehicle) to record any overheard remarks to support a warrant or effect an arrest.

May I wire another person and record the conversations in which he or she engages?

Yes. You may use recording or transmitting devices placed on another person to transmit all conversations of people talking with the wired individual. The court will allow this as being more accurate than testimony of the wired person. You may not, however, place a microphone near a vehicle, phone booth, etc. without the necessary warrant. You could, however, set up a recording device in a nearby vehicle and record all sounds naturally coming to the site.

May I listen in on an extension phone to a conversation?

Yes. You may listen if you have the consent of any of the parties in the conversation. If you do not have the consent of at least one of the parties, you may not listen in without a warrant.

Do I need a warrant to listen to conversations in a motel room or apartment?

You should have a warrant to listen to sounds because the occupants have a reasonable expectation of privacy. You may observe from a public or adjoining area all activity around you and use that or any sounds heard by the unaided ear to support an arrest or warrant.

What if I hear a scream or shot?

You may respond as in any exigent circumstance and enter the premises to insure the safety of others.

Where do I get the sound surveillance warrant?

You should contact your prosecutor to assist you in obtaining the warrant.

B. INFORMANTS

Informants may be used to support search or arrest warrants and, under appropriate circumstances, warrantless arrests. You may stop individuals pursuant to an informant's information to determine the presence of criminal activity.

Informants should be reliable; that is, the information, coupled with past reliability of the informant or other corroborating circumstances, would lead a reasonable police officer acting in good faith to believe that sufficient probable cause exists to proceed with an arrest or seek a warrant. You should obtain information pertaining to the identity of your informant so your can corroborate the basis of your probable cause at a later time.

If, for example, a visitor in a hospital parking lot tells me that the individual in the next vehicle has a weapon in his or her waistband and is selling cocaine from a briefcase, what may I do?

You may **stop** the individual, reach into the waistband (frisk), take the weapon, and, based on that (corroboration), open the briefcase and effect the arrest.

C. OPEN FIELDS

Open fields are the areas outside of occupied premises, and the area immediately around such, including most public space, where a police officer may go freely. You may observe and listen from these areas and use such observations to effect an arrest or support a warrant.

D. PLAIN VIEW

Any evidence, fruits, or instrumentalities of a crime that you observe without your having to move anything, turn anything over, or open anything up may be seized. This "plain view" doctrine requires that (1) you have a legal right to be where you were when you saw the evidence, and (2) you did not have to move or manipulate anything to make the evidence observable. In such cases a "search" has not taken place.

NOTES

CHAPTER 12

ENTRAPMENT

A. DEFINITION

What is entrapment?

Entrapment occurs when a law enforcement official plants in the mind of an otherwise innocent person the inclination to engage in a criminal act. Merely providing the opportunity to engage in a criminal act does **not** constitute entrapment.

Can a person entrapped into committing a crime be convicted of the crime?

No. Generally, entrapment may serve as an affirmative defense in a criminal prosecution. However, the issue of entrapment is a jury decision. This, of course, means that the defendant is admitting that he or she committed the crime.

B. AVOIDING ENTRAPMENT

How do I know when I am merely providing an opportunity for criminal behavior or entrapping a person into committing a crime?

The basic guideline involves the extent to which you are encouraging, prodding, or enticing the person, and providing him or her with the means to commit the crime.

What are some examples of non-entrapment and entrapment?

1. **Non-entrapment**:

   a. In an effort to apprehend the perpetrator of some recent car cloutings (breaking and entering) in a parking lot, police officers park a vehicle with camera equipment in plain view on the front seat. They observe the vehicle from a distance and when someone breaks into it, they make an arrest.

b. In an effort to apprehend a rapist who assaulted several women in one of the parking areas, a female officer poses as a student waiting for a ride. When a person tries to assault her, other officers who have been observing nearby, emerge from their cover and arrest him.

c. To deal with a drug-selling problem, undercover officers act as dealers and as soon as they make a "deal" with a potential buyer, they arrest him.

d. A police officer receives a call about excessive noise at a parking area within a medical center complex. She goes to the location and tells the people to quiet down. She leaves the site but backtracks to see if they have complied. Finding that they are still noisy, she then makes herself known, writes them a citation, and expels them from the area.

e. A female officer poses as a prostitute and asks a person in a port authority bus station if he would like to "have a little fun." The visitor asks "How much?" and she gives a price. When he hands her the money the officer arrests him for solicitation of prostitution.

2. **Entrapment**:

a. Officers hire teenagers to approach the clerk of an airport restaurant and persist in asking him to sell them some beer. The clerk, who has no history of selling alcohol to minors, initially refuses, but after they persist for half an hour, he gives in and sells them a six-pack. The airport police then arrest him for selling alcohol to minors.

b. An undercover officer persists in offering to sell an airport employee some marijuana and, after several minutes of persuasion, the employee finally agrees to buy an ounce, and she is arrested.

93

c. Undercover police officers go to a campus dormitory and persist in attempting to sell alcohol to students in the lounge.

When contemplating any undercover or "sting" operations, remember that, as a law enforcement officer, your policing role consists primarily of preventing, detecting, and investigating illegal behavior, not testing the moral integrity of the people using or working at your facility. For entrapment issues related to drug enforcement, see Chapter 20.

NOTES

CHAPTER 13

FIRST AMENDMENT RIGHTS

First Amendment rights include freedom of speech, press, religion, and assembly; they are among the most protected rights of individuals. The Supreme Court has also recognized the right of privacy to be apparent and emanating from the Constitution.

A. FREEDOM OF SPEECH

1. **Speech**: Freedom of speech is one of the more protected freedoms and generally includes the freedom of expression in most forms. A person has a right to speak in most public locations, though it may be regulated for reasons of real safety under some circumstances. As a note, however, there is no right to be heard. While regulation of the facility will normally accommodate the police officer's needs as well as the people using it, regulations should not be used to exclude unpopular or unpleasant speech.

Obscene language may be dealt with as inappropriate behavior. Language is not obscene, however, merely because it offends particular individuals. The better rule would be to deal with the behavior as being loud or disorderly than merely obscene. As an example, the individual who merely swears at you in your official capacity is not committing an act that, in and of itself, is necessarily criminal.

2. **Expression**: Expression is normally used to act out some conflict with another group or political position. Such expression may include burning books, flags, or figures in effigy. This may obviously be restricted to safe areas (not safe from view or notice only) for fires or subject to fire conditions. Other forms of expression may include sit-ins, vigils, pray-ins, or similar protests. These may be controlled so as not to overflow into other special use areas or for real safety concerns. Again, the control should not develop into unnecessary restraint.

3. **Nudity**: Expression has on occasion taken the form of nudity. The use of nudity as expression may be limited to those demonstrations of value, such as a play, and even then it may be limited to a reasonable display. It is possible not to be obscene in the use of nudity. However, nudity, simply for nudity's sake, is not within the protection of the Constitution and may be banned from public areas.

Does presence at a public facility like a university, airport, port authority or hospital affect free speech or free expression?

First, it must be determined if the location and nature of expression is relevant in terms of time, place and subject of the protest. Generally, protests not identified with the institution may be restricted or prohibited. As an example, a sit-in at the airport to protest plane fares may be acceptable, but a protest against participation in a foreign war may not. A protest blocking access to a university class probably would not be warranted, but a similar protest in front of the administration building or speaker center concerning a controversial speaker on campus may be. A protest in the parking lot of a V.A. hospital concerning lack of adequate funds for veteran medical care may be acceptable, whereas any protest interfering with patient care should not be tolerated.

B. FREEDOM OF THE PRESS

Freedom of the press is very similar to speech. Distribution of handbills, papers, etc. may not be halted in public areas as a general rule. Persons do not have to accept the material, however, and individuals littering may be cited or arrested for such activity, but not for the distribution of the material, *per se.*

C. FREEDOM OF RELIGION

Religious services may be conducted within public facilities so long as they are not dangerous to the participants or others, not unnecessarily intrusive or imposing on others, and within the constraints of the facility's usage. As an example, a religious service may be conducted on the university quadrangle, even if the religion is not conventional. There is no right to compel others to hear or participate in the activities, however, or to use regularly restricted areas of the facility. For example, if an area of the university is closed at midnight, a religious group would not necessarily have a right to enter the closed area for services, without special permission.

D. OFFICIAL ACTION

The notion that certain groups are not "using the facility for its intended purpose" and, therefore, should be removed and kept from interfering with the *bona fide* users is beginning to lose favor with the courts. A balancing of the right of privacy and public use versus compelling state interests seems to be the courts' stance.

As a general rule you, as a police officer, should not deny non-traditional groups the use of the facility if their activities do not truly represent a threat or significant impediment to operations or persons' freedom.

For example, if a group requests a permit to hold a demonstration against the government's policies toward nuclear arms, such a request should not be denied out of hand because it is not in keeping with the facility's "intended purpose." You may, however, be able to restrict some areas and activities of the facility for its protection. As an example, you may keep the demonstrators out of a recently-sodded grassy area to give the grass a chance to grow. You could not, however, exclude the group as individuals from entering an area, provided they meet the appropriate regulations or requirements.

The above comments notwithstanding, persons external to the facility have limited right to enter the facility for purposes of any expression. In this arena, you may have broader authority to restrict such activities than the conventional law enforcement officer.

NOTES

CHAPTER 14

SPECIAL CONSIDERATIONS

A. PURSUIT DRIVING

Although there is no Supreme Court case law that establishes specific guidelines governing law enforcement officers' use of pursuit and response driving, traditional civil litigation in this area has evolved which suggests that the indiscriminate use of pursuit driving may result in an officer's being held liable for any injuries or property damage that results. Because a large proportion of all high speed pursuits engaged in by officers results in injury, the probability of civil litigation is high.

Every police agency should have a vehicle pursuit policy that restricts vehicle pursuits in terms of such variables as: maximum allowable speed, maximum duration, regulations regarding adherence to traffic control signs and signals, type of suspect/offense for which high-speed pursuits are allowed, etc. This policy should be made known to every officer, with the warning that it should be adhered to or the officer will risk the loss of his or her qualified good faith immunity defense, should an incident ever occur that precipitates civil litigation. Similarly, guidelines should be promulgated regarding limitations on other types of response driving (e.g., to an accident, fire, call for assistance, etc.).

As a general rule, high-speed pursuits in the types of facilities addressed in this book are difficult to justify in light of the endangerment they present to the public.

B. DEALING WITH JUVENILES

1. **Juvenile status**: Juveniles, normally persons under the age of eighteen, may be treated differently from adults. Juveniles are always presumed to be in the custody of someone, their parents, a guardian, a person *in loco parentis* (acting in the place of a parent) or some similar relationship.

2. **Custody**: Juveniles in need of supervision for their protection may be taken into custody when there is suspicion or evidence indicating that the child needs care (is dependent and neglected), or is abused.

A juvenile may also be taken into custody if there is suspicion or evidence that he or she is, is about to be, or has been involved in a delinquent act (behavior that would be criminal if committed by an adult) or unruly behavior (acts peculiar to juveniles such as: runaway, truancy, drinking, smoking, out after curfew, etc., depending on the law of the respective jurisdiction).

3. **Officer's options**: Juveniles committing acts that cause police officers to intervene may be dealt with in many ways, but as a rule it should be in "the best interest of the juvenile." Obviously, as an officer, you have more authority to inquire into a youth's age, to inquire into suspicious activity where a juvenile is involved, and to question a juvenile to determine the presence of appropriate adult supervision. You may also counsel or caution the youth or take him or her into custody for any of the appropriate reasons. Of course, you may still act to protect the public as well as the juvenile.

What if I take a juvenile into custody?

If you take a juvenile into custody, you may still be civilly liable for false arrest; however, it is easier to support a need for a juvenile's custody than when dealing with an adult. Paramount in the process is the segregating of youthful offenders from general offender populations and getting them to an appropriate judicial hearing as soon as possible. They must be protected and taken to appropriate authorities quickly.

4. **Constitutional protections**: While juveniles are subject to more restrictions and open to more scrutiny, they are accorded most of the same basic constitutional protections as adults (e.g., an exception would be the right to a jury trial and transcript). This simply means that the need for protection and action in the best interest of the juvenile has been added. A juvenile may be taken into custody (i.e., arrested) in the same manner as an adult. The age of the of-

101

fender will dictate the force and physical restraints that are allowed. A juvenile may be questioned about activities, but the Miranda warnings should always be used where the juvenile is suspected of delinquent (criminal if adult) behavior. As a police officer, you must be sensitive to the needs, fear, confusion, and youthful condition of the juvenile and you should normally assume that the juvenile cannot waive constitutional rights without counsel or the parents or guardians being present.

Probable cause is very important when dealing with juvenile offenders. Mere suspicion is not adequate to support the taking of a juvenile into custody for delinquent or unruly behavior, but may be adequate for an investigative stop even when it would not be for an adult. *Terry* does not specifically identify what is required to make a stop of an adult, and the standard is even less stringent for juveniles because of the requirement to act in their best interest. As a rule of thumb, the adult could leave the mere suspicion scene; however, a juvenile could not. A good rule for you as a police officer is to act in the best interest of the juvenile and in good faith, and you will normally be correct.

Juveniles facing a disciplinary hearing will be accorded the same court procedures and standards of evidence for proof; however, juveniles are not constitutionally entitled to a jury trial in a delinquency hearing. Ordinarily, juveniles at a more advanced age (e.g., over the age of fourteen or sixteen) and charged with more serious delinquent behavior (serious crimes such as murder, rape, armed robbery, or kidnapping) or repeat offenders may be given a waiver hearing by the juvenile court so that they can be tried as an adult.

5. **Contributing to the delinquency of a minor**: If an adult is contributing to the delinquency of a minor, he or she may be arrested on that ground. You should be aware of the appropriate laws of your jurisdiction on this subject. As an example, an adult selling alcohol to a juvenile contrary to the law could be arrested or cited for contributing to the delinquency of a minor in most jurisdictions. Also, an adult accompanying a group of disorderly juveniles in your facility could be cited or arrested if the adult persists in his or her behavior or refuses to make the group conform to appropri-

ate conduct. The juveniles could, of course, be taken into custody for their conduct.

Likewise, in most jurisdictions an adult who is engaging in sexual activity with a (non-spouse) juvenile, is contributing to the juvenile's delinquency.

6. Stopping juveniles:

When I stop a vehicle containing several youths and ask them to empty their pockets and they flee, may I take them into custody?

Yes. The flight under those circumstances is adequate probable cause to take them into custody.

If I approach a group of young people on a blanket on a campus quadrangle and ask if they are having fun and they run, is that adequate probable cause?

No, not without other factors or observations. It would, however, justify a stop and, if warranted, a frisk.

May I ask juveniles found in a public bathroom in my facility what they are doing?

Yes, particularly if there are any supporting circumstances such as smoke, beer cans, liquor bottles, a noisy crowd, etc.

If I see several youths drinking beer may I ask for their identifications?

Yes. You may ask for the identification and follow up with more inquiry of those without proper identification or those under the drinking age. The people should be able to prove that they are adults, unless it is apparent.

May I detain a youthful suspect?

You may detain a youthful suspect more easily than an adult if you have the requisite reasonable suspicion, but you must act more quickly to secure a detention hearing and keep the youth segregated from adults during the detention.

7. Custody disputes involving juveniles. You should have written policy and procedures concerning juveniles and their custody. That policy and procedure should be coordinated with the local juvenile authorities and court.

Generally disputes over custody of a juvenile occur when one parent has legitimate custody and the other does not. In these situations, the parent with legitimate custody and necessary documents to prove such should be allowed actual or temporary custody of any juveniles in the dispute. When conflict arises because of a dispute over custody, regardless of the reasons or the presence of conflicting documents, the juvenile should be placed in the custody of the local juvenile court for a determination of custody, and the resultant court order should be followed. While you may have ample evidence to determine disposition, you do not have to make the determination yourself.

If there is a dispute with an alien or there is a matter of international consequence, the juvenile should be taken into custody, immediately transported to the *local* juvenile court, and the matter referred to the court for disposition.

If a juvenile is traveling alone and becomes confused, disoriented, lost, appears to be a runaway, or is being transported for placement or disposition under the Interstate Compact concerning juveniles, the juvenile should be taken into custody and transported to the local juvenile court or authorities for disposition. Temporarily lost juveniles should, of course, be returned to their parents or guardians unless there is a dispute in any form, in which case the matter should be referred to the local juvenile authorities.

If one parent says, "My spouse is kidnapping my child," what may I do?

You may intercept the parent with the child and the juvenile and inquire into the circumstances. If there is any conflict which cannot be easily resolved, the juvenile should be taken into custody, and the matter should be referred to the local juvenile authorities or court. This is particularly true if the parent with the child is traveling internationally. In that instance the local court should determine the right of custody.

If I find a young child who is lost and wandering around, what may I do?

After a brief, thorough check for parents or guardians, the juvenile should be transported to local authorities for disposition. You should not turn the child over to anyone who cannot prove his or her right of custody. For example, an aunt should be readily identifiable by discussion with the child, the parents on the phone, general information, etc. before the child is permitted to go with her. Do not release the juvenile to some stranger willing to help.

C. DEALING WITH MILITARY PERSONNEL

1. Members of the American Armed Forces

Institutional police are often faced with having to take law enforcement action against someone who is a member of the American Armed Forces. It is important to know that these situations often necessitate special procedures. It is possible that you would not know that a person was in the military, in which instance you should proceed as you would in any other situation. If it becomes apparent to you that a person is in the military, you should proceed as noted below.

May I write a member of the Armed Services a citation?

Yes, if you encounter a person engaging in an act for which you would normally write a citation, even if he or she is on active duty with some branch of the Armed Services, you may write the citation.

May I give a member of the Armed Services a summons to court to answer for violating a law or regulation which I have authority to enforce?

Yes, if you would normally give a summons to an individual for committing the offense, you may give the summons to the member of the Armed Services.

May I arrest a member of the Armed Services?

Yes. As an example, you work in an area near an army base, and you apprehend an off-duty soldier for driving while intoxicated. He tells you that he has to be back at the base in half an hour. You may arrest the individual as you would anyone else.

Once I arrest a member of the Armed Services, is the judicial process any different from what it would be for anyone else?

No. The judicial process for arrest, detention, providing constitutional rights, or care is no different in so far as your actions are concerned. There may, however, be a different process for the military person in the system. If the matter is merely a citation and it is resolved, the matter should be considered closed. If, however, circumstances, either because of impact or seriousness, warrant further action the nearest appropriate prosecutor's office and the nearest military installation (military police or shore patrol) should be notified, giving the charges, name, rank, serial number, military organization, if known, and installation.

2. Members of foreign armed forces

Are members of foreign armed forces treated any differently from members of the American Armed Forces?

No. You should, however, notify the United States Attorney's Office or the United States Department of State of the arrest, including the charges, name, rank and serial number. For example, a foreign navy vessel is moored in a harbor nearby, and you apprehend several sailors on shore leave selling cocaine on a university campus. They should be arrested and the procedures followed as previously noted.

D. ESTABLISHING PROBABLE CAUSE WITH INTOXICATED DRIVERS

With respect to the public's safety, one of the most important enforcement functions you serve is to detect and apprehend people who are driving under the influence of drugs or alcohol. In order to arrest a person for driving under the influence (D.U.I.) and have the person's blood or breath analyzed for the presence of alcohol, you must first establish probable cause that the person is, indeed, D.U.I. In some jurisdictions this is still a relatively easy matter, but because the nation's laws against drunk driving are becoming more punitive, there is also an increasing sophistication among defense attorneys that enables them to more competently discredit you or your testimony when a D.U.I. case reaches trial. In order to present a good case against a drunk driver, it is necessary that you be systematic and thorough in your development of probable cause and in the documentation of your case. Although each court may be different, there are some general guidelines which, if followed, will make it much more difficult for a defense attorney to win a D.U.I. case for his or her client. The following guidelines are presented to help you develop probable cause in a D.U.I. case and then not lose the case when you go to court.

Before you can have a blood or breath test administered to a suspected D.U.I., you must have probable cause that he or she is D.U.I. and effect an arrest based upon your probable cause. You establish your probable cause by observing (1) the suspect's driving behavior, (2) other driver behaviors during your traffic stop, and (3) the driver's performance on selected field sobriety tests.

What are some kinds of initial observations of driver behavior that may be used to raise my suspicions that someone is driving under the influence?

a. weaving or crossing the center line several times,
b. straddling the center line,
c. driving considerably below the speed limit,
d. failing to dim headlights to oncoming traffic,
e. speeding,

f. ignoring traffic signals or signs,
g. littering,
h. excessive use of brakes,
i. turning with a wide radius,
j. following too closely,
k. almost striking another vehicle or object,
l. driving off designated roadways.

During my stop of a potential D.U.I. offender, what types of observations might increase my suspicions?

a. delayed stopping response to your emergency lights or siren,
b. excessive movement of occupants in vehicle,
c. partial roll-down of driver's window,
d. red, watery, or glassy eyes,
e. flushed face,
f. slow or slurred speech,
g. odor of intoxicating beverage (alcohol itself does not have an odor),
h. fumbling in wallet for operator's license,
i. presence of alcoholic beverages in vehicle,
j. delays in responding to requests (e.g., to turn down volume on radio, to provide operator's license or vehicle registration, etc.),
k. excessive belligerence,
l. driver sick/vomiting.

If I suspect that a driver may be under the influence and I attempt to remove him or her from the vehicle, what else should I look for?

a. awkward or unsteady gait,
b. attempts to lean on vehicle for support,
c. difficulty maintaining balance while exiting vehicle,
d. difficulty maintaining balance while standing,
e. indications of stomach sickness, vomiting, etc.

If I continue to suspect D.U.I. and want to administer field sobriety tests, what points are relevant to developing probable cause for an arrest?

1. Before using any field sobriety tests, you should (a) be trained in their administration by an expert, and (b) have an opportunity to practice executing them and administering them. Remember, you will probably be asked to demonstrate these tests in court.

2. Demonstrate each test you plan to administer just prior to administering it.

3. Administer more than one test (at least three would be preferable).

4. If driver fails any test, give him or her at least two more chances to perform it.

5. Record the order of tests given.

6. Record the number of attempts that driver made to pass each test.

7. Record the specific way in which driver failed each test.

8. Remember to make note of any statements the driver may make about speech impediments, inner ear infections, medication, or other conditions that may affect his or her balance or test performance.

What are some of the generally accepted field sobriety tests?

Several different types of tests have been developed and, before deciding on the ones you will use, it is a good idea to find out which ones are preferred by the prosecutor(s) and judge(s) who may be dealing with your D.U.I. cases. Below is a list of some of the more commonly accepted field sobriety tests:

1. Tests of balance:
   a. one leg stand test: driver stands on one leg, holds other leg straight out in front, about six inches off the ground for 30 seconds (driver counts slowly to 30 while looking at the raised foot),
   b. heel-to-toe test: driver walks a real or imaginary straight line heel-to-toe for nine steps, pivots slowly on the left foot, and walks back nine steps; driver counts the steps out loud and watches his or her feet while walking,
   c. heel-to-toe/pick-up-coin test: driver walks heel-to-toe for about nine steps, bends over to pick up a coin from the ground, and then stands up straight,

2. Tests of coordination: Finger-to-nose test: driver shuts eyes, tips head back, extends arms out to side and then attempts to touch nose by first placing the index finger of one hand then the index finger of the other, on nose.

3. Tests involving speech:
   a. recite the complete alphabet, preferably by beginning with some letter in the middle such as "G".
   b. counting-fingers test: Using one hand only, driver counts fingers while simultaneously touching thumb to the four fingers, beginning with the little finger, going to the index, and then counts backwards beginning with the index and going to the little finger. Thus, the counting sequence is "one, two, three, four, four, three, two, one," and the appropriate fingers must be touched. When driver finishes with one hand, he or she then counts fingers on other hand in same manner.

4. Horizontal gaze nystagmus test: This test is based on the fact that alcohol impairment usually affects the eyes' ability to efficiently follow objects moving back and forth in a horizontal plane. The driver is asked to hold his or her head still while visually following a moving object (e.g., a pen) as the officer moves it back and forth in front of the driver's face.

What information should be included in the incident report that I will take to court?

In addition to the standard information, you should include the following:

1. your initial observations that led you to make the traffic stop,

2. any significant observations about how the violator responded to your request to "pull over,"

3. any relevant observations about the violator's physical and verbal behavior, odors, liquor in the vehicle, etc. when you first made your contact,

4. any relevant observations about how the violator acted or what the violator said when he or she exited the vehicle,

5. what field sobriety tests you administered, the order in which they were given, how many times each was attempted, whether they were passed or failed and, if they were failed, in what specific ways they were failed,

6. any other observations about the violator's behavior that may be relevant, e.g., general demeanor, vomit, belligerence, statements about drinking, etc.

What if a suspected D.U.I. refuses to take a field sobriety or a blood or breath test?

Most states have "implied consent" laws which means that a refusal to take the test results in loss of driving privileges for a certain period of time. However, it is important to remember that you may be able to successfully prosecute a D.U.I. case based upon your general observations of the driver's behavior before and during the traffic stop as well as on other evidence that may be available (e.g., open liquor bottles). In other words, in the case of uncooperative drivers, the results of field sobriety tests or blood or breath samples are not necessarily required for conviction. Clearly, in such cases, as well as all D.U.I. cases, the quality of your observations and report will be critical.

E. MODEL INVENTORY POLICY

It shall be the policy of _____ to inventory all private or abandoned property that is impounded, regardless of reason. This policy is to be followed in its entirety by all personnel. The purpose of the inventory procedure is to protect any valuable property that may be part of an impoundment and protect the institution from the possibility of negligence in the loss of private property. The inventory procedure is **not** to be used as an alternative to obtaining a search warrant in those cases in which it is suspected that evidence of criminal activity may be present with the impounded property.

Inventorying impounded vehicles: When any vehicle is impounded by police, it will be completely inventoried and will include the passenger compartment, the glove box, the trunk, the spare tire well, ashtrays, and any unlocked or unsealed containers, regardless of size. Examples of containers would include, but are not limited to, such things as: backpacks, handbags, purses, film canisters, flashlights, wallets, picnic baskets, athletic bags, camera cases, glasses cases, diaper bags, luggage of all types, tool boxes and kits, first aid kits, plastic or paper bags, tackle boxes, shoes, boots, rifle and pistol cases, cardboard boxes, etc. Any containers that are locked or sealed (e.g., with strapping tape) will be inventoried as single units, without opening them. Wheel covers and hubcaps will be removed and placed in the trunk to secure them. The engine area will be checked for anything of special value (e.g., chrome parts).

When the inventory is complete, all items of value will be secured, and a written record of everything of value will be made and signed by the inventorying officer(s).

Inventorying non-vehicles: In the event that other property is impounded (e.g., boats, camping equipment, camera equipment, backpacks, handbags, etc.), a complete inventory will be made and will include inventorying all unlocked or unsealed containers. Each locked or sealed container will be inventoried as a single unit without opening it.

When the inventory is complete, all items of value will be secured, and a written record of everything of value will be made and signed by the inventorying officer(s). All property found and in custody of the police department that was not obtained pursuant to a seizure will be inventoried.

Evidence: If, during the inventory procedure, evidence or fruits or instrumentalities of a crime should be inadvertently discovered, the inventorying officer(s) shall stop the inventory immediately, secure the property being inventoried, maintain the chain of custody of the found evidence, and notify supervisory personnel. The purpose for this procedure is to allow a decision to be made as to whether to seek a warrant to search the impounded vehicle or property.

F. Diplomatic Immunity

Persons whom you have detained for committing violations of institutional regulations or committing crimes on facility property and who claim diplomatic immunity may be held to verify their diplomatic status. In such cases it is your responsibility to immediately contact the United States Department of State to verify their claim. Follow the instructions of the appropriate State Department authority. During this time treat the individual(s) with respect and care and do not conduct a search of their persons or property. You may, of course, frisk to protect yourself or others, if warranted. You should also notify the United States or State's Attorney of the person's identity and the offense. If the matter is minor, you should consult your supervisor. The person with diplomatic immunity may be merely cited or expelled from the facility and the same authorities notified.

G. Special Law Enforcement Incidents

Some institutional police departments have developed S.W.A.T. teams to handle special situations requiring heavy law enforcement intervention. To avoid potential exposure to liability for negligent activities related to the management of such incidents, the skill and training level which the team brings to an incident must be at least equal to that possessed by other area teams which could otherwise be called to handle the situation. As an example, if an airport police S.W.A.T. team responds to a hostage situation, its equipment, training, and the quality of its leadership's decision making should be comparable to that which the S.W.A.T. team from the local municipal police department would possess.

The underlying rule is that the police department may not deprive the public of the best available policing techniques and skills.

In any case, police department members not trained in S.W.A.T. tactics should **never** function as S.W.A.T. team members. Furthermore, all S.W.A.T. activities, including training, should be driven by written policy and procedure.

Police management must operate with an awareness that S.W.A.T. teams may tend to over respond because of the exigencies of the crisis. Thus, management should carefully temper any response in these situations.

Of course, the same requirements would hold for a police department's involvement in hostage negotiations, handling bomb threats, dignitary protection, etc. This would include the requirement for written policies and procedures.

In any bomb threat situation, unless you are absolutely sure that the bomb does not exist, individuals in the area should be immediately evacuated to safety before any other action occurs.

NOTES

CHAPTER 15

AN OVERVIEW OF LIABILITY

Concern over liability issues has been the driving force behind major changes in law enforcement procedures, selection standards, training, deployment, supervision and retention. In fact, it is fair to say that it has been the primary driving force behind law enforcement reform in general. In spite of its importance, however, many law enforcement practitioners are relatively unaware of the nature of liability and liability exposure and how these concepts impact the law enforcement function in institutional settings. What follows is a review of these concepts and the categories of liability.

What is legal liability?

Legal liability is the responsibility a person has under law for his or her actions or inactions.

What is legal duty?

Legal duty can be defined as that which a person is legally obligated to do or refrain from doing. Generally, a person has a duty to exercise reasonable care to avoid subjecting other persons or their property to unreasonable risks of harm.

Legal duty may also be that which one should do, based on the probability or foreseeability of injury to a party. As public servants, police officers have imposed on them a duty that they must meet for ethical and professional reasons. Carrying out this legal duty will also reduce their exposure to liability.

What is the "public duty doctrine"?

The "public duty doctrine" refers to a duty owed by a law enforcement officer to the public, as a whole, to provide for the general safety and welfare; it is not owed to any particular individual as such. As an example, airport police have a general duty to remove drunk drivers from airport roads.

What is a "special duty" owed to an individual?

A "special duty" is a duty owed to a particular individual or class of individuals that results from a special relationship. For example, there is a special duty incumbent on an officer to remove a person incapacitated in the middle of a roadway to a place of safety. The special duty is imposed on the officer because of the duty and the resultant training and skills to provide for safety for those unable to secure their own.

In a civil lawsuit what options for obtaining relief are open to the plaintiff?

a. *Injunction*: the plaintiff may sue to have the defendant cease an action.

b. *Commence action*: the plaintiff may also sue to have the defendant begin an action (e.g., put up a fence).

c. *Damages*: the plaintiff may sue to obtain a monetary judgment from the defendant to "balance the wrong" of some act. *Direct damages* cover direct losses as a result of the negligent act and compensation for such things as pain and suffering. *Punitive damages* are sometimes awarded in addition to direct damages as a "fine" the defendant has to pay to the plaintiff as a result of some grossly negligent, willful, or reckless act that inflicted the loss or injury.

What are the various categories of liability, and how are they defined?

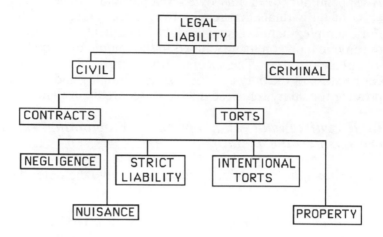

Legal liability may be divided into two main categories: *criminal* and *civil.*

***Criminal Liability*:** Criminal liability is the culpability or responsibility for an act or failure to act that has been defined by law as a harm against the state. The violation of criminal laws amounts to an act against the state (as well as the person who was the actual victim of the act). In other words, in criminal liability, it is the state (public as a whole) which has been wronged.

***Civil Liability*:** Civil liability is the culpability or responsibility for an act or failure to act that caused a loss or harm to another individual, but is not considered to be a wrong against the state.

What are the categories of civil liability?

There are two principal types of civil liability:

a. Liability involving **contracts.**
b. Liability involving **torts**. This category would be of most interest to those in policing.

What is a tort?

A **tort** may be thought of as a loss or a harm sustained by a person that provides the legal basis for a lawsuit.

Are there different types of torts?

Yes. Torts may be divided into the following types:
a. Negligence
b. Strict liability
c. Intentional torts
d. Nuisance torts
e. Property torts

What is "liability" in tort law?

Liability in tort law is a creation of individual case decisions, commonly referred to as the common law. Generally, conduct may be tortuous only if there is a legal duty to act or avoid an act, which results in injury. No jurisdiction has attempted to completely codify this area of law. Accordingly, when we talk about tort law we do so without definition; we are, nonetheless, seeking principles and rules to avoid liability.

Perhaps the easiest way to understand this law is to recognize that it is a part of civil law, i.e., it is concerned with what the individual can do to find remedy for an injury sustained from the action or inaction of another party. Remember, however, that a civil wrong may also be a criminal wrong and, therefore, punishable by the state.

What is the purpose of tort law?

There are three purposes in this area of law:
1. Compensate the victim: in so far as possible to "make whole" the victim, as much as the money paid in damages can.
2. Provide justice: by requiring those responsible to pay the determined damages.
3. Deter others: society is made safer by deterring dangerous behavior which creates injury.

What is required to demonstrate tort liability?

Liability requires the following four elements:
1. A **duty** owed to the injured party by the party responsible for the injury.
2. A **breach** of that duty because of the action or inaction of the party responsible for the injury.
3. An **injury** to the party to whom the duty was owed.
4. A **causal connection** between 2 and 3 above.

What is meant by "proximate cause"?

Proximate cause is a legal fiction used to limit a defendant's liability. It requires that the injury has a reasonable relationship to the tortuous conduct. As a rule, one must consider whether the consequences of the act were foreseeable and whether or not intervening causes exist. Normally, liability is limited to individuals who were in the foreseeable area of hazard and where the foreseeability was present when the injury took place.

A defendant, therefore, may be liable if he or she could have foreseen any harm from his or her actions or lack thereof. Furthermore, the defendant may be liable even if it was not foreseeable, unless the court finds that the likelihood that the conduct would cause the resultant harm was too remote or unusual.

NOTES

CHAPTER 16

TORT LIABILITY: NEGLIGENCE

What are the different types of torts?

The categories of torts include negligence, nuisance, strict liability, intentional torts and property.

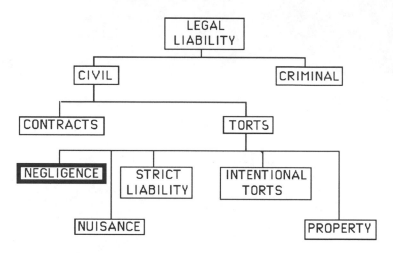

What is Negligence?

Negligence is an act or failure to act that results in loss or injury to an innocent party. Negligence is conduct (whether intentional or not) that fails to conform to legal standards. A jury makes a determination of negligence by asking whether a defendant's conduct was the same as the fictional "reasonably prudent person," if placed in the same circumstances.

Must I be perfect?

The law requires no one to be perfect but only that he or she act as the reasonably prudent person would in a similar situation. The reasonably prudent person is generally one with normal or average attributes. However, in cases in which people must possess more knowledge or higher qualifications, skills, or intellect than the average reasonably prudent person, they may be held to the higher level. Police officers would fall into such a category, and they must exhibit the appropriate standard of care.

What is meant by "standard of care"?

Standard of care (in negligence cases) represents the level of care a reasonable person of similar skills and qualifications would use under similar circumstances. It is the criterion by which courts evaluate behavior; the fictional "reasonable person." The resultant standard of care is normally couched in terms of "ordinary care," "due care," or "reasonable care." Implicit in this legal doctrine is the notion that the standard of reasonableness is not normally met if a person engages in an act or failure to act that results in an injury or loss to someone else. Reasonableness implies that if the person either *knew or should have known* that his or her behavior could be the proximate cause of injury to another, and an injury occurs, then an acceptable standard of care is not met.

Thus, a defendant's liability for an injury is founded upon what he or she knew or should have known of a risk, and that a sufficient degree of probability is present that will cause a harm to a plaintiff. An officer must understand the parameters of reasonableness as applicable to his or her duties under the law. No provision is made for any weaknesses of an officer, so any forgetful, careless, ignorant, foolish, rash, impetuous, timid, or clumsy person is held to the "reasonable person" standard whether he or she can conform or not.

How are standards of care established?

Standards of care are often created by case law, guidelines for juries, legislative histories, legislation, and rules of law, but are generally left to juries. Generally, the violation of a law (statute) is negligence *per se*, which means that if the defendant fails to introduce evidence which excuses the violation, the negligence as to the defendant is conclusively established.

Give some examples of reasonably prudent conduct and adequate standard of care.

a. An officer would be held to a requirement of competency with firearms or first aid techniques. The knowledge of the use of firearms within the facility, under all weather conditions and times of the day, would be the assumed reasonably prudent level. The officer would be assumed to know more about first aid procedures than the average lay person; however, a doctor would be presumed to conform to an even higher standard. Furthermore, once you assume the role and begin carrying out a duty, you must follow through with the appropriate standard of care. Failure to do so may result in a finding of negligence.

b. Generally, police officers would be expected to have increased capacity to anticipate emergencies and respond to them. As an example, in a very heavy rain storm, police officers should automatically remove people from potential flood areas or respond adequately if caught by a surprise flood. The fact that a flood has not occurred before is not a defense; the question is how the reasonably prudent person with an officer's skills would respond.

c. One is supposed to reasonably anticipate or foresee some types of conduct of others. The officer, in particular, is supposed to foresee circumstances in which he or she can expect negligent or criminal conduct by others or in which the officer may instigate behavior in a person that would subject others to risk or harm.

What are the different degrees of negligence?

The popular degrees of negligence are **slight, ordinary,** and **gross.**

Slight negligence is a failure to exercise slight care.

Ordinary negligence is the failure to meet the mythical "reasonable person" standard of care.

Gross negligence is a failure to exercise great or unusual care.

Some conduct is more dangerous than others and requires a special duty. Those responsible for dangerous instrumentalities must exercise a higher degree of care or reasonableness under the particular circumstances. A police officer disposing of a bomb would fall in this category.

What is reckless conduct?

Reckless conduct (sometimes referred to as willful and wanton misconduct) occurs when a person knew or should have known that his or her conduct creates an unreasonable risk of harm and the risk, in degree or probability, is relatively high that harm will occur. In reckless conduct a defendant must be conscious that the conduct creates a relatively high risk of harm, as opposed to negligent conduct in which no awareness of risk is required. However, reckless conduct lacks the certainty of outcome found in intentional torts.

With respect to negligence, what is required to demonstrate the existence of liability?

The plaintiff carries the burden of proof and must demonstrate, with a preponderance of the evidence, the following:

a. There was a legal duty to perform, with respect to another person, in a certain way or to certain standards.

b. There was a breach of that legal duty to perform.

c. There was some loss or injury sustained by the victim of the negligent act or failure to act.

d. The negligent performance was the proximate cause (i.e., in the direct causal chain) of the loss or injury.

Again, what is proximate cause?

Proximate cause is something which, in natural unbroken sequence, produces a result and without which the injury could not have occurred. It is the cause of an accident or injury. It is, however, not necessarily the closest thing in time or space to the injury and not necessarily the event that set things in motion. The notion of proximate cause is very important because, for liability to be established, it is a requirement that the defendant's actions be a proximate cause of the loss or injuries.

What is "res ipsa loquitur"?

Res ipsa loquitur: The "thing speaks for itself" rule is one of circumstantial evidence. If a plaintiff can show that his or her injury was (1) caused by an instrumentality or condition which was under the exclusive control or management of the defendant, (2) under circumstances in which the plaintiff's injury would not have occurred unless the defendant was negligent, and (3) that the plaintiff did not cause the injury-causing incident, then the jury may assume, without further proof, that the defendant's conduct was negligent and therefore the cause of injury. As an example, when a plaintiff is able to demonstrate that he or she was placed unconscious in a patrol car behind the screen with the doors closed, and should not have sustained a broken arm, but did, the jury may assume that the officer was negligent and therefore liable, unless the officer is able to prove something else was the cause.

What are some of the variables affecting negligence liability?

a. *Contributory negligence*: Contributory negligence asserts that a plaintiff's conduct was such that it created an unreasonable risk of harm to the plaintiff when combined with the defendant's negligence. In most jurisdictions, contributory negligence mitigates rather than negates liability. Normally, contributory negligence is not a defense if the defendant's conduct falls in the reckless conduct and strict liability categories.

128

Comparative negligence: Comparative negligence generally allows a distribution of liability and, therefore, of damages, between the plaintiff and defendant.

c. *Last clear chance*: When a plaintiff (or his or her property) is in a danger from which he or she cannot extricate him- or herself, and the defendant has an opportunity to prevent the harm, the defendant is not permitted to use the plaintiff's prior negligence as a defense to negate his or her own negligence.

d. *Assumption of risk*: In most jurisdictions, if a plaintiff voluntarily assumes the risk of harm that arises from a defendant's reckless or negligent conduct, he or she may not recover for the particular harm. The risk must be assumable and the potential harm apparent. There appears to be a trend toward restricting this defense.

What is vicarious liability?

In negligence cases, **vicarious liability** allows a person (and a legal entity) to be liable for another's behavior when a relationship to supervise, aid, or train exists, and the supervisor either knew or should have known that the conduct of the subordinate would be likely to result in harm to another. As an example, if a police supervisor was aware that another officer under his or her authority tended to be abusive, and the officer was brutal in the handling of an arrestee, the supervisor and entity could be found liable for the injury. The ability to remedy the matter is in the hands of the supervisor; therefore, the liability is imputed to the officer and the entity.

In some jurisdictions employers are liable for all conduct of their employees while acting within the scope of employment, whether the employer knew or should have known of the likelihood of the harm.

The department and supervisors most often will be placed in a position of liability for the acts of officers if the officers are acting within the color of law. The scope of employment factor is a question for the jury and they may take into consideration any factors having a bearing on the employment relationship.

129

NOTES

CHAPTER 17

TORT LIABILITY:
STRICT LIABILITY, INTENTIONAL
TORTS, AND NUISANCE

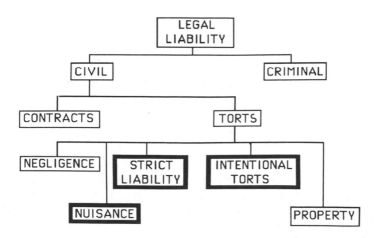

A. STRICT LIABILITY

What is strict liability?

Strict liability refers to situations in which a person may be held liable even though the person exhibited reasonable care and did nothing "wrong." Having to "make good" on a product that turned out to be defective would be an example of strict liability.

While strict liability may be imposed in other areas, in a public institution it is routinely associated with abnormally dangerous activity. Factors that may be associated with the rule are:

1. What is the extent of risk? That is, how high a degree of risk of harm exists, and what is the likelihood that the harm to others will be great?

131

2. Is there an ability to eliminate the risk? If the risk remains after reasonable care is taken to avoid it, the possibility of strict liability may still exist.

3. Is it an abnormal activity? The further away from common usage, the greater the exposure to strict liability.

4. Location: Is the activity being conducted in an improper place?

5. Societal interests: Does the activity's value exceed its social value?

What are some limitations on strict liability?

a. Proximate cause requires the harm to result from the abnormal danger for liability to be established.

b. Legislative action may preclude strict liability, or legislation authorizing one to carry on the activity will normally exclude strict liability. Legislation may also create strict liability in certain situations.

B. INTENTIONAL TORT

What is an intentional tort?

An **intentional tort** occurs when the loss or harm caused by the action or inaction was intended by the person inflicting the tort.

What is intent?

Intent is a desire to cause a particular consequence by a specific act or the belief that the end result is a substantial certainty of the act.

Examples of Intentional Torts

What is a battery?

Battery is offensive physical contact with another or with something in his or her immediate control or possession. Something as simple as knocking off a hat could be a battery.

What is assault?

If a person intentionally places another in apprehension of an imminent battery, an **assault** has occurred. There must be an intent to cause the contact; the plaintiff must be aware (apprehension) of the act before its termination; and there must be an apparent intent and ability to carry out the threat at that time.

As an example, a visitor firing a weapon at another, but missing, does not commit an assault unless the person at whom the shot was directed is aware of the incident and, therefore, apprehensive of the shot. This is distinguished from criminal assault, which does not require knowledge or apprehension on the part of the intended victim, because the action is viewed as being against the public as a whole (sovereign). Furthermore, assault requires that no privilege to use force exists. For example, a campus police officer physically expelling a rowdy party from a college dorm would not generally be liable for an assault.

What is false imprisonment?

The intentional confinement of a person by an individual, absent legal authority, is **false imprisonment**. As an example, the detention by an officer of an individual for shoplifting in an airport shop could be false imprisonment, absent probable cause for arrest or statutory relief permitting a brief detention for investigation.

What is intentional or reckless infliction of emotional distress?

A defendant is subject to liability to a plaintiff for **emotional distress**, or resulting harm, that is caused by extreme and outrageous behavior he or she intentionally performed. Abuse of power by a law enforcement officer which exceeds the ordinary means of persuasion or demand is designated as a flagrant abuse of power in the nature of extortion and, as such, may be actionable.

What are the defenses to liability for intentional torts?

a. *Privilege*: As a rule privilege is found by consent or an act of law, irrespective of consent. For example, a police officer is privileged to use reasonable force to apprehend an individual.

b. *Consent*: When one is willing for the conduct to occur, there is consent which is almost always a defense to any tort. For example, a person consents to battery in a football game, but this does not extend to excessive force which would exceed the consent.

c. *Self defense and defense of others*: A person is normally privileged to use reasonable force as is necessary to protect him- or herself from immediate physical harm threatened by the intentional or negligent conduct of another person. This includes the use of self defense against an assault, false imprisonment, or a negligently caused harm. Excessive force is not permitted, and any force used after the person extending the original conduct is subdued, disarmed, helpless, or has withdrawn from the fracas is not permitted.

Likewise, force may be utilized to come to the defense of another under the same circumstances that the third party would be privileged to defend him- or herself against. However, if the intervening defender is wrong, that mistake, no matter how reasonable, is irrelevant, and the defender may be liable for assault, battery, etc.

134

A person with a duty to protect another person or his or her property is privileged, under law, to use reasonable force or confinement, appropriate to the occasion, to effect the duty.

d. *Defending and recovering property*: One in possession of property may utilize reasonable force to expel another from or prevent trespass on property or prevent the taking of personal property. This is true even though the force used would normally be an assault, battery, or false imprisonment. Only necessary force is permitted, and any force likely to cause death or great bodily harm is not permitted.

One may use limited self-help to recapture one's property wrongfully and forcibly taken from one's possession, even where there is a claim of right, or if obtained by fraud or duress. The effort to recapture the property must begin immediately upon the dispossession or after learning of it so that it is a continuous, uninterrupted act. Demand to return the property must be made first. Then, if the demand is futile, only reasonable force, not force likely to cause serious bodily harm, may be used. Mistake as to the need for the force is no defense to liability.

e. *Necessity*: The defense of necessity may be utilized when defending one's person or property from some harm in a manner that results in harm to the plaintiff. Public necessity will be the defense which a police officer would most often use. For example, a police officer sets a back fire to stop a fire encroaching onto airport property, and the fire burns another's house; it would frequently be excused so long as the reasonable care standard is met. The danger affects the airport (in this case) or the community so that public interest is involved and, therefore, the privilege is allowed.

f. *Authority of law*: Individuals acting under the authority of law are privileged, under appropriate circumstances to commit acts that would normally be assault, battery, imprisonment, and trespass. A police officer could, therefore, physically restrain (battery) an individual,

135

handcuff him or her (confinement), and transport the person to the station, if it is in furtherance of reasonable law enforcement.

Ministerial v. discretionary acts: A police officer, using appropriate discretion, may in good faith determine how to act (e.g., whether to arrest or close an area of the hospital grounds) and is privileged so to do. Ministerial (obligatory) acts, on the other hand, are not in the privileged category, regardless of good faith, if done improperly.

C. NUISANCE

What is an action for nuisance?

Nuisance refers to conduct, and generally is identified as either *public* or *private*. Private nuisance, a particular activity or thing which unreasonably and substantially interferes with a person's enjoyment of property, is normally of little consideration in public institutional settings. Public nuisance, on the other hand, is an unreasonable interference with a common collective right. Generally, this includes interference with public peace and safety, health and comfort, and public morals. These rights must be common to the public.

NOTES

CHAPTER 18

TORT LIABILITY:
OTHER LIABILITY CONSIDERATIONS

A. LIABILITY CONSIDERATIONS FOR EMPLOYERS AND EMPLOYEES

Does the employer-employee relationship generate any special concerns?

The employer-employee relationship creates liability for and toward one another.

1. *Vicarious liability*: An employer may be vicariously liable for the acts of his or her employee if the employee was acting within the scope of his or her employment. As noted previously, the department and supervisors most often will be placed in a position of liability for the acts of officers if the officers are acting within the color of law. The scope of employment factor is a question for the jury and they may take into consideration any factors having a bearing on the employment relationship.

2. *Intentional torts*: If an employee is acting within the scope of his or her employment, and intentionally commits a tortuous act in furtherance of the employment, the employer is vicariously liable. Where there is a special duty of protection between an employer and a plaintiff, the employer may be vicariously liable for an injury in breach of that duty, whether committed in furtherance of the employer's interest or for personal reasons. For example, if there is a medical emergency call from the airport concourse and the officer does not respond, the employer inherits the responsibility.

3. *Direct liability*: The employer may be directly liable, not vicariously liable, for the conduct of the employee. Most often the employer may be directly liable for such

acts on his or her part in selecting, hiring, training, instructing, testing, supervising, evaluating, retraining, reassignment, etc. The employer may also be directly liable for the consequences of commanding or authorizing an employee's act.

In general, to escape liability, employers must provide a safe place to work with safe equipment or tools adequate for the job, with adequate competent fellow employees, under adequate supervision, and with training necessary to accomplish the work.

B. LIABILITY AND CONTRACTORS

How does the use of independent contractors affect liability exposure?

As a rule, an employer is not vicariously liable for physical harm caused by an independent contractor or its employees. However, there are exceptions to this rule, which include such things as: negligent standards and contract minimums, selection, instruction, failure to inspect and monitor work, retention of control and supervision, and duties of special relationships.

C. LIABILITY INVOLVING INTERFERENCE WITH FEDERAL CONSTITUTIONAL RIGHTS

Persons interfering with another's constitutional rights under color of law may be sued under 42 U.S.C. § 1983. (See Chapter 2 section on Civil Liability).

D. MISREPRESENTATION AND DEFAMATION

What is negligent misrepresentation?

An erroneous misrepresentation about another, even if honestly believed to be true, is actionable if it fails to meet professional or business standards, and there is a failure to exercise reasonable care in determining the truth.

What is defamation?

Generally, a false statement about another intentionally disseminated to others may provide a cause for litigation. There are two types: *libel* and *slander*. **Libel** is the written word defaming another, while **slander** is the publication by any other means.

E. A POLICE OFFICER'S IMMUNITIES TO LIABILITY

As a police officer, what protections do I have from exposure to liability?

In addition to some of the issues already discussed above, the following protections should be mentioned:

1. *Good faith*: Good faith involves individual performing responsibilities with good intentions. *Qualified, good-faith immunity* refers to the fact that a person performing in good faith at the "reasonable person" standard or better generally will be found not liable for his or her actions performed within the scope of his or her duties.

2. *Statutory relief*: An act granting relief or limits on liability may occur in some jurisdictions to protect certain activities of law enforcement officers.

3. *Governmental (or sovereign) immunity*: Common law immunity has been abolished or narrowed in all jurisdictions of the United States. Most states and the United States have tort claims acts allowing individuals to seek relief or restitution from the government.

4. *Information and training*: The most effective defense against liability is proactive measures—adequate information and training. This includes adequate training, continual maintenance of skills and current information relating to one's duties and responsibilities. As an example, a police officer performing within the reasonable standards of the profession will normally avoid engaging in activities that produce harm.

Insurance: Liability insurance can be invaluable. It will allow the officer to work in good faith without fear of serious repercussions. Officers should be alert to the exemptions in coverage provided by an insurance policy. It frequently exempts the carrier from paying damages or providing counsel for incidents resulting from criminal behavior, violations of civil rights, and activities outside of the scope of employment or outside of the jurisdiction. Normally, punitive damages are also excluded from coverage.

NOTES

CHAPTER 19

SPECIAL TOPICS IN LIABILITY:

TRAINING, DRIVING UNDER THE INFLUENCE ENFORCEMENT, AND RIDE-ALONG PROGRAMS

A. LIABILITY IN LAW ENFORCEMENT TRAINING

One of the growing liability areas in law enforcement concerns the notion of **training negligence**. The courts have held that under certain circumstances, the victim of some police abuse, misconduct or other action may take civil action against the officer and his or her entity if the officer's behavior is a product of negligent training. This type of suit often involves civil rights law (i.e., 42 U.S.C. §1983) but could also stem from other liability avenues.

What makes law enforcement training "negligent"?

Whether or not training is negligent is determined on a case-by-case basis. In general, it would have to be demonstrated that the training does not meet currently acceptable standards within the law enforcement training community, omits important aspects, is not adequately documented, is not taught by experts in their fields, or contains inadequate standards for the trainee's successful completion. Like many areas of the law, the standards for training negligence are still evolving; thus, the prudent law enforcement manager, trainer or practitioner would be well advised to take a proactive approach toward the issue and insure that law enforcement training and in-service training programs are professionally conducted.

What can I expect to face in training negligence litigation?

There is no way to predict accurately what will happen in any given courtroom when you are facing litigation over law enforcement training practices. In general, however, you can expect that the plaintiff's attorney has researched the particular area of training that is at issue. He or she has gone to established experts in that particular type of training and discovered what the "state of the art" is with respect to the issue at hand. The attorney will utilize the process of discovery which will include questioning you and others outside of court before trial and will subpoena your training records.

Should my department have a training officer system?

A well designed and implemented training officer program is invaluable to introduce the new officer to the responsibilities of policing. The selection, training and duties of the training officer should always be taken seriously to reduce exposure to liability. The training officer's role is to insure that the recruit exhibits the knowledge, skills, and abilities required of the job, and to participate in the final screening before the recruit is permanently employed.

What specific steps can I take to reduce my exposure to liability related to training practices?

Although this question cannot be answered completely, the following guidelines will help trainers to evaluate their programs and trainees to assess the training in which they are asked to participate.

1. Is there a complete course syllabus and lesson plan which you can produce on demand?
2. Are there complete attendance records on every student in every class which you can produce on demand?
3. Are the instructors experts in the areas they have been assigned to instruct? Can you document their expertise?
4. Are the resource materials, books, and training aids current, appropriate, and related?
5. Where special instructor certifications are generally the norm (e.g., firearms, CPR, etc.), do the instructors hold them?
6. Are copies of the course quizzes and exams available for inspection?

144

7. Are records of each student's performance available for each testing situation?
8. Do the testing procedures preclude cheating?
9. In firearms training, do the trainees qualify
   a) with the particular weapon(s) they carry?
   b) with the particular ammunition they carry?
   c) with their weapons under reduced illumination as well as in daylight?
   d) within the times allowed by the timed courses of fire (i.e., or are they allowed to shoot "alibis"?)
   e) with a shotgun, if they have access to one?
10. Has the program ever failed a student? If not, how are you going to demonstrate that the program maintains any standards?
11. To what extent is the purported length of the program inflated in terms of the actual number of training hours given?
12. Does the program contain any role-play or situation training component through which you have an opportunity to assess students' interpersonal and technical skills as they attempt to apply them in law enforcement settings?
13. Do you and your trainers understand the importance of identifying and reporting any trainees who, because of their behavior, lead you to believe that they possess personality traits that make them unsuited for the law enforcement role (e.g., tempers, racism, etc.)?
14. If you are employing officers who were trained by someone other than yourself, have you investigated the training program and are you satisfied that it meets all the above standards?
15. Do you provide for periodic in-service law enforcement training programs, and does the content of these programs address perceived needs or inadequacies that may arise among your law enforcement personnel?
16. Are your training officers selected and trained with care, and do you have a written policy detailing the structure and function of the training-officer program?

What these 16 areas amount to is a checklist against training negligence. Clearly, a potential avenue for a plaintiff to get into the "deep pockets" of an institution is to maintain that the mistreatment, injury, or loss he or she received from one of its officers resulted in part from incompetent or inadequate law enforcement training and supervision. An effective training program can minimize this threat.

B. Managing the Intoxicated Driver

A question often facing institutional police officers is what to do with drivers who have been drinking alcoholic beverages. Should they be arrested and transported to jail? Should they be driven home? Should they be told to park by the side of the road or in a parking lot for an hour to sober up? Should a sober occupant of the vehicle be identified and given responsibility for driving it? What if a person under the influence is stopped and released? What is the liability picture if such a driver subsequently inflicts injury to him- or herself or to a third party?

Although the law is still evolving on this point, under some circumstances it may be possible to hold an officer liable for injury or loss sustained by a third party who was injured by an intoxicated driver who was stopped by the officer shortly before, but allowed to continue driving.

What is the "Public Duty" Doctrine?

The public duty doctrine holds that an officer's duty is to the general public and not to any specific person, unless a "special duty" has been created.

Doesn't this doctrine protect me from liability resulting from a third party injured by a drunk driver whom I have previously stopped and released?

It is true that this doctrine implies that the failure to restrain an intoxicated driver, where the driver subsequently causes harm to a third party, allows the third party no cause of action. The law enforcement officer's historical duty is to the general public and not to a specific individual; however, this duty is being redefined and expanded in the courts. In some of the cases dealing with the failure to restrain, the courts

146

decided in favor of the public duty doctrine, maintaining that a duty to the individual plaintiff did not exist.

In other cases, however, the doctrine was set aside and the officers or their entities were found liable. The courts' reasoning in some cases favoring the plaintiff held that a special duty to protect individuals from drunk drivers was created by statutes spelling out police duties to enforce drunk driving laws.

How do the concepts of discretionary and ministerial function apply to the release of intoxicated drivers?

Discretion (discussed earlier) may be defined as "the power to act within general guidelines, rules, or laws, but without either specific rules to follow or the need to completely explain or justify each decision or action." *Ministerial* implies that acts are done by carrying out orders rather than by making choices of how to act. *Ministerial functions* are activities that are absolute, fixed and certain, and in the performance of which there is no discretion. They are done by carrying out a general policy rather than by setting or making policy.

Because officers, and their entities, are traditionally immune to liability stemming from discretionary acts, the outcome of a case may center on whether the court considers an officer's decision to arrest a drunk driver to be discretionary, denying liability, or ministerial, implying liability.

What is the best alternative when I stop a driver whom I consider too intoxicated to drive?

In general, the best alternative is to arrest the driver and transport him or her to jail. This strategy precludes the possibility of the driver harming him- or herself or someone else. Of course, any given situation may call for a different solution, but you should be aware that it may also create a potential for greater liability frontage.

147

C. LIABILITY AND RIDE-ALONG PROGRAMS

Many institutions are faced with requests from non-commissioned employees as well as from members of the public to ride along with a police officer during his or her tour of duty. Also, occasions may arise when the administration invites various members of the public to ride along with a patrol officer. These situations often create questions for managers regarding liability, should the passenger become injured as a result of the activity.

What must I do to reduce liability exposure in these ride-along situations?

a.   Ride-along programs should require that such passengers accompany only experienced officers possessing good skills, techniques, and judgment.

b.   Legal expertise should be consulted to develop a *hold-harmless agreement* (release) to mitigate any damages ensuing from an incident. The agreement should include acknowledgement of the potential harms that may be encountered in the company of a law enforcement officer, as well as a statement clearly intending to hold harmless the officer, supervisors, and entity in the event of an incident. It should be recognized that, although they are recommended, hold-harmless agreements are of limited value.

c.   As a rule, it is wise for the entity to acquire insurance to cover potential damages and litigation expenses.

NOTES

CHAPTER 20

SOME LEGAL ASPECTS OF
DRUG ENFORCEMENT

How would I know that my institution has a drug problem that should be addressed?

There are several possible indicators:
a. incidents of drug overdoses
b. incidents of drug-related violence
c. identification of individuals clearly under the influence
d. reports from local and state narcotics officers that the facility is used as a transaction area
e. discovery of drug paraphernalia by employees
f. discovery of illegal drugs growing on facility property
g. observations of probable drug transactions between members of the public
h. reports from the public that drug use is occurring in the institution

What strategies are available for managing a drug problem?

There are fundamentally only two strategies available to management for carrying out such a mission: (1) The first approach is to discover the source of the drugs and attempt to reduce the supply to the public or employees by identifying the producers and dealers and interdicting the transportation and supply. (2) The second approach is to target the users or buyers of illegal drugs and to intervene in a way that will reduce the likelihood that they will use or purchase drugs again in the facility. For either of the above approaches, some covert activities will probably be necessary to accomplish the mission.

What techniques are available to target the dealers and/or users of illegal drugs?

One technique would entail the use of undercover officers "hanging around" likely locations for drug activity, perhaps attempting to buy drugs from suspected dealers, keeping notes, and possibly seeking warrants for any dealers who may be identified. The problem with arresting any given drug dealer is that the drug-dealing niche he or she has occupied will immediately be filled by some other dealer.

A second approach incorporates the technique known as the **reverse sting**. In reverse stings, police officers or informants posing as drug dealers make drug sales and then, together with backup undercover officers in the immediate area, arrest the buyers. To maximize safety, these teams are carefully trained and follow a highly structured procedure for making contacts with potential buyers, completing a sale, and then effecting an arrest. Each team member has a specific job to do and acts in total coordination with the other members. Procedures for these activities have been worked out and field tested by numerous law enforcement agencies.

Is it legal for law enforcement officers to sell drugs?

This question has been addressed many times and legal opinions and case law indicate that the answer is "yes." 21 U.S.C. § 841(a) makes it a federal offense to distribute a controlled substance. However, it is generally held that an officer is not criminally liable in this situation because his or her behavior lacks the necessary element of criminal intent. In addition to the legal tradition that would exempt an officer who sells illegal drugs in a reverse sting, federal drug law exists that specifically provides this immunity in 21 U.S.C. § 855(d).

Can reverse sting operations be considered entrapment?

Entrapment occurs when a law enforcement official plants in the mind of an otherwise innocent person the inclination to engage in a criminal act. Merely providing the opportunity to engage in a criminal act, however, does not constitute entrapment.

In the implementation of successful reverse stings, *predisposition* of the potential defendant will remain the critical

151

element should he or she, when prosecuted, claim entrapment. To avoid a court ruling that the officer overstepped his or her duties by inciting or creating the crime, the officer should remain a neutral salesman and allow the buyer's predisposition to control the transaction. It may be considered entrapment for the law enforcement officer to encourage or lure a customer with overly zealous selling techniques into buying something the customer doesn't want.

What are some guidelines for reducing the risk of entrapment?

a. When officer-sellers solicit business, they should not mention words such as "crack," "coke," "dope," "grass," "ice," or any other illegal drug.

b. Officers should not attempt to encourage a person to buy from them if, at first, he or she denies interest in a drug purchase.

c. Specific people should not be selected for an extra intensive selling effort. The courts have held that targeting specific individuals for sting activities requires a reasonable suspicion that they are likely to engage in the crime. Remember, in the type of "reverse-sting" operation being discussed here, it is not the individual as much as the activity that is being targeted.

What steps are involved in setting up a reverse-sting drug operation?

a. First, it may be necessary to educate those in authority about reverse stings and explain their value in addressing the issue of drug abuse at the particular facility site. Such an attempt will probably include reassurances about the legal aspects of reverse stings, as well as reassurances regarding the public relations implications of such programs.

b. Similarly, the local court and prosecutors with whom the institution works will have to be brought into the planning discussions.

c. Other area law enforcement agencies should also be contacted and brought into the planning. One valuable strategy (where jurisdictions overlap) is to involve some of these other officers in the reverse stings, thus taking advantage of their experience and sharing with them and their agencies the kudos associated with such undertakings.

d. Where feasible, trustworthy sources in the local media can be contacted and briefed on the plan so that when it is put into operation, there is an increased potential for effective, positive press coverage of what the institution is trying to accomplish.

e. The selection of the reverse-sting team is clearly a critical component to the program's success. Reverse stings are highly orchestrated operations in which every participant knows exactly what his or her role will be. Each position has a specific name and associated responsibility, and there is a "play-book" by which everyone functions. Members should be volunteers who are physically in shape and adequately trained in self-defense and arrest techniques.

f. The reverse-sting team must undergo an adequate amount of briefing and scenario training to give the members experience with what they are going to say, how they are going to act as a team, and what they will do should unique types of situations arise. It is wise to videotape this training to provide additional feedback to the participants.

g. With respect to the drugs that will be sold, decisions have to be made as to their type and sources of supply have to be obtained. Although the particular drugs employed may vary from area to area, most sellers will probably find that it will be necessary to provide cocaine, crack cocaine, and marijuana. With the approval of the court, arrangements can be made through local, state, and federal narcotics enforcement to obtain the drugs. Of course, an accounting system will have to be established.

h. In situations in which buyers use motor vehicles to arrive at the selling site, these vehicles may be confiscated. As part of the reverse-sting planning, a procedure (manpower) will be necessary for removing these vehicles from the scene.

153

i. Locations for potential reverse stings must be identified and evaluated for their appropriateness. Such factors as exposure to the public, possible escape routes, locations for back-up positioning, and personal safety of the officers, the buyers, and the visiting public must all be taken into account and incorporated into the plan. Also, intelligence must be gathered as to the typical *modus operandi* of drug dealers in the area so these strategies may be duplicated.

NOTES

GLOSSARY

Accessory After the Fact: An accessory after the fact knows that the felony has been committed and gives aid and comfort to the felons by assisting in their escape, or avoiding detection or arrest.

Accessory Before the Fact: An accessory before the fact is a person who aids, counsels, directs, or orders the commission of a crime but is not present at the time the actual crime is committed. These persons may also be principals in the second degree.

Administrative Arrest: Administrative arrests are based on the same general requirements as conventional arrests and, therefore, they depend on the same foundation. The administrative arrest is different because of its dispositional character rather than its probable cause foundation.

Administrative Frisk: You may frisk a person entering a facility, consistent with institutional guidelines, because the person may be carrying prohibited items, or materials dangerous to the institution or its personnel.

Adult: A person who has reached his eighteenth birthday, unless declared otherwise by law.

Affidavit: A sworn statement.

Arraignment: The accused is called before the court to hear the formal charges against him and enter a plea.

Arrest: Taking a person into custody or depriving a person of the freedom to come and go because he is a suspect in a particular crime.

Assault: A threat to do bodily harm.

Attempt: An attempt to commit a crime is the action of preparation, but just falling short of completion. An attempted murder may involve injury but does not result in death.

Bail: A sum of money set by the judge to insure that the accused will show up and submit to trial.

Battery: The unlawful touching of another, frequently used with assault.

Bench Warrant: A warrant issued from the bench (i.e., a judge in court).

Burden of Proof: The responsibility of the prosecution to prove the accusation with sufficient evidence and, in a criminal case, to establish guilt beyond a reasonable doubt.

Chain of Custody: The protected and documented progression of evidence from the time it is seized until it is admitted at trial. An adequate chain of custody insures the trustworthiness of the evidence.

Change of Venue: The transfer of a court case from one location, such as a county, to another. The motion is made where it appears the venue location is prejudicial or inflamed and the defendant would be denied a fair trail.

Charge: The accusation for which a person is held and tried.

Civil Action: A civil, as opposed to criminal, legal proceeding in which a party seeks some remedy such as money, damages or an injunction.

Color of Law: The figurative cloak or mantle of authority of a public official to carry out the functions of his or her office. It allows a person to act in an official capacity.

Common Law: The law that is derived from the historical customs and court decisions based on those customs as opposed to statutory law.

Competency: The judge will determine the fitness of a witness to testify in a trial or the fitness of documentary or physical evidence to be admitted.

157

Competent: In criminal matters, the ability to understand the nature and seriousness of the charges and the ability to assist in one's defense.

Complaint: A sworn statement alleging a crime by a particular person.

Conduct: Conduct, in the eyes of the law, includes acts and failure to act.

Consent: A waiver of a constitutional right given with the knowledge of the right not to do so. It must be given freely, intelligently, and without coercion.

Conspiracy: An agreement between two or more people to commit a crime.

Contemporaneous: Occurring at the same time and place.

Contempt of Court: Willful disobedience of a court order.

Continuance: The postponement of a court proceeding to a later date.

Contraband: Property that may not be lawfully possessed and may be lawfully taken by an officer for that reason. This does not normally include real estate.

Corpus Delicti: The object upon which the crime was committed, such as the body of a murder victim or the shell of a boat that was burned.

Credibility: The jury's decision of whether a witness is credible, believable.

Criminal Intent: The criminal intention to knowingly and willfully engage in the criminal act, which is required to establish guilt. Reckless conduct may suffice to demonstrate intent, as may negligent behavior.

Cross-Examination: The in-court questioning of a witness for the opposition to determine the truthfulness and accuracy of the testimony that he or she gave.

Curtilage: The close space around a dwelling that is considered part of the dwelling and is the premises in which there is the highest reasonable expectation of privacy. It is the space that would be found within the "picket fence," and includes close out buildings in which a man or woman could stand, such as a barn, corn crib, chicken house, etc.

Damages: The money compensation awarded the plaintiff in a civil action for an injury or loss. Compensatory damages are for the actual loss or injury, while the punitive damages are over and above that amount to punish the offender and deter repetition of the harmful act.

Delinquent: A juvenile who has committed a crime.

Detention: The temporary holding of a person for the purpose of investigation. The action is for a very short period and does not constitute an arrest.

Double Jeopardy: The United States Constitution prohibition of the prosecution of a person for the same crime by the same jurisdiction more than once unless the matter is appealed by the accused.

Dual Sovereignty: The situation in which a crime offends more than one jurisdiction (sovereign), such as federal and state and either or both could prosecute without violating prohibitions of double jeopardy.

Due Process: The constitutionally guaranteed protections and procedures preventing loss of life, liberty, or property without such proper legal safeguards.

D.U.I.: Driving under the influence, i.e., being under the influence of some intoxicant or drug.

D.W.I.: Driving while intoxicated, which in most jurisdictions is driving while intoxicated by some drug or alcohol.

ith alcohol, it is generally a blood level of at least 0.08% r 0.1% by weight depending on the jurisdiction.

Elements of a Crime: Certain elements which must be proven to convict a person of any particular crime. As an example, the elements of burglary (common law or first degree in most states) are the (1) breaking and (2) entering, of the (3) dwelling of (4) another (5) at night, with the (6) intention of committing a felony. All of the elements must be proven plus the fact that the accused did the acts at the time and place stated.

Elephant Rule: The area in which an officer may search, which is confined to the place of need or the place where the item sought is likely to be. If searching for an elephant, you may not look in the glove compartment. If you are searching for narcotics, on the other hand, a glove compartment would probably be an appropriate place to look.

Entrapment: The defense that the accused did the act but that the only reason was that the law enforcement officer tricked or persuaded him to do so. The theory is that the evil intent originated in the mind of the officer who was trying to entrap the accused.

Evidence: The testimony or tangible objects introduced in a trial to convince the jury or judge of the truth of a fact at issue.

Exclusionary Rule: A judicially created rule that allows the defendant or court to suppress (exclude) for trial any evidence, or derivatives thereof, obtained illegally by governmental officers or agents acting under color of law.

Exigent Circumstances: Unusual circumstances allowing quick action where such is not normally permitted. A scream, a shot, the probability that evidence is about to be destroyed immediately, the presence of great immediate danger, etc. are examples.

Ex Post Facto: The United States Constitution prohibition of an action being made a crime after it occurs. It also prohibits the increasing of a penalty for the crime after the act.

Extenuating Circumstances: Facts concerning the commission of a crime that may reduce the punishment. This does not excuse the crime; it may only lessen the penalty.

Extradition: The legal process by which one jurisdiction obtains a person for prosecution from another jurisdiction holding the person.

False Arrest: The unlawful detention or holding of a person.

Felony: A serious crime for which the punishment is normally a year or more in prison.

Frisk: A pat down of outer clothing for the purpose of looking for weapons and based on the belief that the suspect may be armed or dangerous. The pat down includes all external clothing and is not a search.

Fruits of a Crime: Items gained from the commission of a crime, e.g., money from the bank robbery.

Fruit of the Poisonous Tree: Otherwise legal and proper evidence obtained as the product of other illegal police activity which is not, as a rule, admissible.

Grand Jury: A group of citizens taken from a cross section of a community by law to hear the presentation of some evidence in a case and determine if there is sufficient probable cause to indict. If the Grand Jury determines that there is sufficient probable cause it hands down an indictment.

Habeas Corpus: A petition by one who believes that he is being held in jail illegally and demanding that the holding authority justify the detention or release him.

Had Reason to Know: An individual, normally a defendant, had such information that a person of at least reasonable intelligence would derive that a particular fact exists.

Harm: When considering liability, a measurable injury to a person, property, or interest.

161

Hearsay: A statement by one witness of what he heard another person say.

Indictment: The formal written charges against an individual on which the person is brought to trial. The indictment is handed down by the Grand Jury.

Initial Appearance: The first judicial hearing for the accused for the purpose of determining detention, bond or both.

Injury: In discussing liability, an injury is some type of intrusion upon an interest protected by tort law.

Insane: A legal term dealing with the suspect's mental state at the time the offense was committed. A person may be found not guilty by reason of insanity. The theory holds that the insane person's mental state prevented his having the evil intent to commit the act.

Intoxication: Having one's behavior influenced by some chemical such as alcohol. Normally, voluntary intoxication is not a defense to a crime.

Judicial Notice: The judge taking notice of a fact without its having to be proved (e.g., it is dark at midnight).

"Jump and Reach" Rule: The search area immediately around the arrestee where the person in custody might "jump and reach" a weapon or destroy evidence.

Jurisdiction: The authority to inquire into a crime, deal with it through arrest and trial, and pass sentence.

Juvenile: A person who has not reached his eighteenth birthday, unless declared otherwise by law.

Mala in Se: Crimes which are naturally wrong in themselves such as murder, rape, kidnapping, burglary and robbery.

Mala Prohibita: Crimes created by law which are wrong because the acts impose on others or interfere with the orderly operation of society. Examples would be: speeding, illegal parking, and walking on the grass.

Malice: The criminal intent or state of mind causing the person to commit the crime.

Mere Suspicion: A hunch, or a feeling based on the officer's experience that something is amiss, which may cause the officer to observe or investigate further. It is not the basis for further action until additional articulable facts elevate the suspicion or knowledge.

Minor: Generally a person who has not reached his eighteenth birthday, unless declared otherwise by law.

Miranda Warning: The Court-mandated warnings that must be given to a suspect prior to in-custody interrogation. These warnings include: (1) the right to remain silent, (2) the right to have an attorney present during interrogation, (3) the right to have a court-appointed attorney if the suspect cannot afford one, and (4) anything the suspect says can be used against him or her in a court of law.

Misdemeanor: A less serious crime for which the punishment is normally less than a year in prison.

Mistrial: A trial which is incomplete because of a deadlocked jury or procedural error. The trial may be held again without double jeopardy interfering.

Modus Operandi, also M.O.: The pattern or way of doing something. In criminal matters it normally refers to the pattern of committing the crime by a particular individual or group.

Moving Roadblock: An officer on patrol stopping vehicles or persons in vehicles matching a particular description or a particular need such as permit checks, license checks, etc.

Motive: The reason a person committed the crime.

Negligence: An act or omission of an act that causes harm to another which the reasonably prudent person would not do. This occurs in criminal and civil matters.

Open Fields: The areas outside of a curtilage in which an owner's expectation of privacy is diminished.

Perjury: A statement made under oath in a judicial proceeding, which the person making the statement knows to be false.

Physical harm: In liability, a term which implies abuse of the person or property of another.

Plaintiff: The party bringing suit in a civil action.

Plain View: Items which an officer may observe without moving objects or entering an area in which he or she does not have a right to be. Objects may be observed with the aid of a flashlight, binoculars, etc.

Plea: The accused enters a plea before trial, normally guilty or not guilty or *nolo contendre*. A plea of "guilty" is a total admission to all of the facts of the charge to which it is entered. A "not guilty" plea is a total denial of all facts. The *"nolo contendre"* is a denial for civil purposes but an admission for criminal purposes (I didn't do it and I won't do it again).

Preliminary Hearing: A judicial hearing to determine probable cause to hold an accused and set bail.

Presumption: An inference at law that a fact exists because of another fact.

Presumption of Innocence: A presumption that all persons are innocent even though charged with a crime. This presumption lasts throughout the trial process until the jury returns a verdict of guilty. The state must overcome this presumption by proving beyond a reasonable doubt that the accused committed the particular crime as charged.

164

Principal: Principals are designated principals in the first or second degree. A principal in the first degree is the person who actually commits the crime. If more than one person commits the crime, all are principals in the first degree. A principal in the second degree is normally absent at the time the crime is committed but aids in the actual commission.

Probable Cause: In arrest, the existence of more reason to believe than not that a particular person committed a particular crime.

Reasonable Suspicion: The belief by an experienced reasonable officer that a crime is about to be, is being, or has been committed (short of probable cause to support an arrest) which gives the officer the grounds to stop, and frisk if appropriate, an individual for a brief investigative time to determine the circumstances and determine if probable cause does in fact exist.

Search Warrant: A court order directing an officer to search a specified location, person or object for particular evidence of a suspected crime and to seize such evidence if it is found.

Self Defense: The defense in a court proceeding that the accused had to use the force in question to defend himself and that he had a right to do so.

Search (of a person): A search conducted pursuant to a warrant and within the scope of the warrant or incident to an arrest. The search incident to arrest is to protect the officer, prevent the destruction of evidence, and prevent escape or suicide.

Search (of an area): The search for particular evidence, contraband, fruits, or instrumentalities of a crime pursuant to (a) a warrant and within the scope and time frame of the warrant, or (b) a search of the immediate surrounding area ("jump and reach" rule) of an arrestee, which is permitted pursuant to the arrest if contemporaneous in time and place.

Should have Known: An aspect of negligence, which holds that a person of reasonable intelligence would know of a particular fact or set of facts and govern his or her behavior accordingly.

Specific Intent: The requirement in some crimes of the proof of specific intent to commit the crime or cause the result, which cannot be presumed from the unlawful act itself.

Statute: Laws enacted by the legislative body and signed into law by the presiding executive, governor, or president.

Statute of Limitations: A statutory creation of a time limit in which an indictment must be filed or the crime may not be prosecuted. Statutes of limitation vary from one jurisdiction to another, but as a rule the more serious crimes are not included and may be prosecuted at any time.

Subpoena: An order of the court commanding the appearance of a person to give testimony and to bring certain objects if so ordered.

Suppression Hearing: A judicial hearing to determine whether or not evidence should be suppressed under the Exclusionary Rule because the evidence is incompetent.

"Terry" Frisk: A frisk that had judicial approval in the case *Terry v. Ohio*; that is, a pat down of outer clothing for the purpose of looking for weapons and based on the belief that the suspect may be armed or dangerous. The pat down includes all external clothing and is not a search. See cases for further information.

Tort: A wrongful act or failure to act which causes injury or loss to another and for which the injured party may sue for damages or injunction.

Unruly Behavior: Behavior peculiar to juveniles that is contrary to law, such as drinking, smoking, being out after curfew, etc.

Venire: The group of citizens from which a jury is drawn.

Venue: The location or site of the crime.

166

Verdict: A finding by the judge or jury after all of the evidence has been presented.

VIN: Vehicle Identification Number. A number required by law and normally on a plate assigned to a particular vehicle. The number is easily observed and accessible to view and, if covered, may be cleared for viewing by the officer.

RELEVANT LEGAL CASES

ARRESTS

Warrantless Arrests

Payton v. New York, 445 U.S. 573, 100 S.Ct. 1371, 63 L.Ed. 2d 639 (1980): The Fourth Amendment prohibits police from making a warrantless and non-consensual entry into a suspect's home (or premises) in order to make a routine felony arrest. Entry may be made without a warrant only if the officer is in hot pursuit or there are exigent circumstances.

United States v. Watson, 423 U.S. 411, 96 S.Ct. 820, 46 L.Ed.2d 598 (1976): Failure to secure a warrant for an arrest will not invalidate the arrest if it is based on probable cause.

California v. Hodari D., ___ U.S. ___, 111 S.Ct. 1547, 113 L.Ed.2d 1547 (1991): If a suspect does not yield to a show of authority, and there is no physical force, there is no seizure of the person. There must be an application of force, however slight, or a show of authority to which a suspect submits, for there to be a seizure of the person.

Hearings

County of Riverside v. McLaughlin, 114 U.S. 49, 111 S.Ct. 1661, ___ L.Ed. 2d ___ (1991): A jurisdiction that has probable cause determination must do so as soon as reasonably feasible, but no more than 48 hours after the arrest.

BAIL:

Stack v. Boyle, 342 U.S. 1, 72 S.Ct. 1, 96 L.Ed. 3 (1951): Bail is excessive if it exceeds the amount necessary to insure the accused's presence at trial.

168

COUNSEL:

Brewer v. Williams, 430 U.S. 387, 97 S.Ct. 1232, 51 L.Ed.2d 424 (1977): The police may not interrogate once an accused has refused to speak without his attorney being present.

Brown v. Mississippi, 297 U.S. 278, 56 S.Ct. 461, 80 L.Ed. 682 (1936): Confessions obtained by coercion are a violation of due process.

Escobedo v. Illinois, 378 U.S. 478, 84 S.Ct. 1758, 12 L.Ed.2d 977 (1964): Incriminating statements made during an interrogation in which requests for counsel were denied and Miranda warnings were not given are inadmissible at trial.

Gideon v. Wainwright, 372 U.S. 335, 83 S.Ct. 792, 9 L.Ed.2d 799 (1963): An accused is entitled to counsel in a trial.

Massiah v. United States, 377 U.S. 201, 84 S.Ct. 1199, 12 L.Ed.2d 246 (1964): An accused's incriminating words obtained after charges had been filed during an interrogation without benefit of counsel may not be introduced against him in trial.

Spano v. New York, 360 U.S. 315, 79 S.Ct. 1202, 3 L.Ed.2d 1265 (1959): A confession obtained through fatigue and sympathy is involuntary and inadmissible.

DEADLY FORCE:

Tennessee v. Garner, 475 U.S.1, 105 S.Ct. 1694, 85 L.Ed.2d 1 (1985): Deadly force may not be used to effect an arrest. Deadly force may be used only where the officer has reason to believe that the suspect poses a significant threat of death or serious injury to the officer or to others.

ELECTRONIC SURVEILLANCE, INFORMANTS, AND AGENTS:

Hoffa v. United States, 385 U.S. 293, 87 S.Ct. 408, 17 L.Ed.2d 374 (1966): Evidence obtained from a secret informer is valid if the evidence is given voluntarily and based on "misplaced confidence."

Katz v. United States, 389 U.S. 347, 88 S.Ct. 507, 19 L.Ed.2d 576 (1967): A person with a reasonable expectation of privacy is protected by the Fourth Amendment, and a physical trespass without a warrant is a breach of that privacy.

Lewis v. United States, 385 U.S. 206, 87 S.Ct. 424, 17 L.Ed.2d 312 (1966): An agent, under cover, may deceptively enter a premises that has become a commercial center (i.e., selling narcotics) without a warrant and all observations and conversations are legal seizures.

United States v. White, 401 U.S. 745, 91 S.Ct. 1122, 28 L.Ed.2d 453 (1971): The Fourth Amendment does not apply where a person voluntarily confides wrongdoing. A person's expectations of trust are not protected.

ENTRAPMENT:

United States v. Russell, 411 U.S. 423, 93 S.Ct. 1637, 36 L.Ed.2d 366 (1973): The question of entrapment is for the jury, which will assess the defendant's predisposition to commit a crime rather than the type or degree of police conduct.

EXCLUSIONARY RULE:

Mapp v. Ohio: 367 U.S. 643, 81 S.Ct. 1684, 6 L.Ed.2d 1081 (1961): Affirmed the Exclusionary Rule; evidence obtained improperly (in this case, without a valid search warrant) may not be used against a defendant in court.

Segura v. United States, 468 U.S. 796, 104 S.C
3380, 82 L.Ed.2d 599 (1984): The Exclusionary Rule doe
not apply if the connection between illegal police conduct,
discovery, and the resultant seizure of evidence is so
"attenuated as to dissipate the taint."

FIRST AMENDMENT:

A Quaker Action Group v. Morton, 516 F.2d 717
(1975): Although some facilities may be reserved for specific
purposes, in general, public assembly for First Amendment
purposes is a justifiable "park use."

GOOD FAITH:

Malley v. Briggs, 475 U.S. 335, 106 S.Ct. 1092, 89
L.Ed.2d 271 (1986): This case explored the limits of qualified good-faith immunity to alleged Fourth Amendment violations. Even though he had a warrant, the officer was liable
for an unconstitutional arrest because he should have known
that the facts presented for the warrant did not establish
probable cause. Officer must exercise reasonable professional judgment.

SELECTED FIFTH AMENDMENT CASES

Coercion

Arizona v. Fulminante, ___ U.S. ___, 111 S.Ct. 1246,
113 L.Ed.2d 302 (1991): Whether or not a confession is coerced depends on the totality of the circumstances; if, however, a defendant's confession is coerced, its use against the
defendant will be reviewed from the beginning (*de novo*)
under the harmless error rule.

Informing Suspects of Their Rights

Beckwith v. United States, 425 U.S. 341, 96 S.Ct.
1612, 48 L.Ed.2d 1 (1976): Miranda is not applicable to a
non-custodial interrogation that is voluntary in nature.

rkemer v. McCarty, 468 U.S. 420, 104 S.Ct. 3138, *** L.Ed.2d 317 (1984): Before questioning, Miranda *arnings must be given to a suspect taken into custody, :ven for a traffic violation.

Colorado v. Spring, 479 U.S. 564, 107 S.Ct. 851, 93 L.Ed.2d 954 (1987): As long as they are Mirandized, subjects of custodial interrogation do not have to be informed in advance of the subject of the interrogation.

Illinois v. Perkins, 496 U.S. 292, 110 S.Ct. 2394, 110 L.Ed. 2d 243 (1990): A law enforcement officer posing as an inmate need not uncover his or her identity by giving Miranda warnings to a jail suspect before asking questions that may elicit an incriminating response regarding an uncharged crime.

Miranda v. Arizona: 384 U.S. 436, 86 S.Ct. 1602, 16 L.Ed.2d 694 (1966): Established the standard for advising suspects of their constitutional right to counsel and against self incrimination before any custodial interrogation by law enforcement officers takes place. The warning is to include the fact that the accused will have counsel appointed for him at no expense to himself if he cannot afford counsel and that he need not answer questions until he has consulted with counsel.

Moran v. Burbine, 475 U.S.412, 106 S.Ct. 1135, 89 L.Ed.2d 410 (1986), Police have no duty to inform an in-custody suspect about to be questioned that his lawyer is in another room and wants to consult with him.

New York v. Quarles, 467 U.S. 649, 104 S.Ct. 2626, 81 L.Ed.2d 550 (1984): Miranda warnings are not required in urgent or exigent circumstances where there is an overriding concern for public safety.

Oregon v. Elstad, 470 U.S. 298, 105 S.Ct. 1285, 84 L.Ed.2d 222 (1985): After a suspect is informed of the Miranda warnings and makes a voluntary statement, the statement may be used.

Oregon v. Mathiason, 429 U.S. 492, 97 S.Ct. 711, 5{ L.Ed.2d 714 (1977): Miranda warnings are required where a suspect has been deprived of his freedom so as to render him in custody, but not for others who may be questioned.

Orozco v. Texas, 394 U.S. 324, 89 S.Ct. 1095, 22 L.Ed.2d 311 (1969): Miranda warnings must be given any time a person is being interrogated and is deprived of his freedom in any way.

Pennsylvania v. Muniz, ___ U.S. ___, 110 S.Ct. 2638, 110 L.Ed. 2d 528 (1990): The absence of Miranda warnings does not prevent the admission, at a drunk driving trial, of the bulk of the video tape recording of the responses and comments uttered by a defendant while he was being tested for sobriety and booked.

Right to Counsel

Minnick v. Mississippi, ___ U.S. ___ 111 S.Ct. 486, 112 L.Ed. 2d 489 (1990): Officials may not reinitiate interrogation of an accused without counsel present after the accused has requested and been provided counsel. The Fifth Amendment protection is not terminated or suspended when the suspect has consulted with an attorney.

INEVITABLE DISCOVERY:

Nix v. Williams, 467 U.S. 431, 104 S.Ct. 2501, 81 L.Ed.2d 377 (1984): Even though evidence would have been suppressed due to a violation of Miranda warnings and lack of counsel, the evidence will not be suppressed when the police did not act in bad faith in a separate search and where it was inevitable that the evidence would be discovered from an independent source.

INVENTORIES:

Colorado v. Bertine, 479 U.S. 367, 107 S.Ct. 738, 93 L.Ed.2d 739 (1987): Inventories of impounded vehicles may include any unsealed container found inside the vehicle, as ɔng as the inventory is done in good faith and not for the ɔurpose of obtaining evidence. Law enforcement officers do not have to offer an arrestee the opportunity to make his or her own arrangements for securing the vehicle; they may impound the vehicle if they wish.

South Dakota v. Opperman, 428 U.S. 364, 96 S.Ct. 3092, 49 L.Ed.2d 100 (1976): A vehicle taken into police custody for protection of the vehicle may be inventoried pursuant to standard police procedures without a warrant.

Florida v. Wells, 495 U.S. 1, 110 S.Ct. 1632, 109 L.Ed.2d 1 (1990): Opening a closed container encountered in a vehicle inventory violates the Fourth Amendment, absent a written policy directing such activity. In no event may the inventory be used as a pretext for uncovering evidence.

JURISDICTION:

Solorio v. U.S., 483 U.S. 435, 107 S.Ct. 2924, 97 L.Ed.2d 364 (1987) The military has jurisdiction over an active duty service member accused of a crime, even if the crime is not service-connected.

JUVENILES

In re Gault, 387 U.S. 1, 87 S.Ct. 1428, 18 L.Ed.2d 527 (1967): While verifying the philosophy for dealing with juveniles, Gault establishes four guarantees for juveniles in the juvenile justice process 1) Notice of charges; 2) Right to Counsel; 3) Right to confrontation and cross-examination; and 4) the Privilege against self-incrimination.

Kent v. United States, 383 U.S. 541, 86 S.Ct. 1045, 16 L.Ed.2d 84 (1966): A juvenile is entitled to a hearing, which may be informal, prior to waiving a juvenile over to be tried as an adult. While the hearing need not conform to all the requirements of a criminal trial or even the usual administrative hearing, it must measure up to the essentials of due process and fair treatment. It includes as a minimum, the right of counsel and the incidents thereto.

New Jersey v. T.L.O., 469 U.S. 325, 105 S.Ct. 7
83 L.Ed.2d 720 (1985): The Fourth Amendment's prohib
tion concerning unreasonable searches and seizures applie
to searches conducted by school officials. However, ac-
commodation of privacy interests of school children with the
substantial need of teachers and administrators for freedom
to maintain order in schools does not require strict adherence
to the requirement that searches be based on probable cause
to believe that the subject of the search has violated or is violating the law. Rather, the legality of the search of a student
should depend simply on reasonableness, under all of the
circumstances, of the search.

In the Matter of Winship, 397 U.S. 358, 90 S.Ct.
1068, 25 L.Ed.2d 368 (1970): Juveniles, like adults, are
constitutionally entitled to proof beyond a reasonable doubt
when they are charged with a violation of criminal law.

LINEUPS:

Kirby v. Illinois, 406 U.S. 682, 92 S.Ct. 1877, 32
L.Ed.2d 411 (1972): There is no right to counsel at a lineup
before the accused is arrested or charged.

Neil v. Biggers, 409 U.S. 188, 93 S.Ct. 375, 343
L.Ed.2d 401 (1972): A suspect's rights have been violated
and the evidence obtained from a lineup may be excluded
when the lineup is unduly suggestive.

United States v. Wade, 388 U.S. 218, 87 S.Ct. 1926,
18 L.Ed.2d 1149 (1967): Once an accused has been formally
charged he is entitled to counsel at a lineup.

PROBABLE CAUSE:

Draper v. United States, 358 U.S. 307, 79 S.Ct. 329,
3 L.Ed.2d 327 (1959): Probable cause exists when an officer of reasonable caution believes that an offense is being or
is about to be committed, based on objective facts and circumstances.

Illinois v. Gates, 462 U.S. 213, 103 S.Ct. 2317, 76 L.Ed.2d 527 (1983): The rigid "two prong test" is abandoned in favor of the "totality of the circumstances test" when determining whether an informant's tip will support probable cause for the issuance of a search warrant. A warrant may be issued on a partially corroborated anonymous informant's tip.

PROTECTIVE SWEEPS:

Maryland v. Buie, 494 U.S. 325, 110 S.Ct. 1093, 108 L.Ed.2d 276 (1990): Police officers need no more than a reasonable suspicion to conduct a protective "sweep" of a dwelling in which they are making a valid arrest.

SEARCHES:

Consent Searches:

Florida v. Jimeno, ___ U.S. ___, 111 S.Ct. 1801, 114 L.Ed.2d 297 (1991): Consent to search a vehicle extends to closed containers found inside of the vehicle that could contain the object of the search. However, it does not normally extend to locked or sealed containers, unless specifically incorporated in the consent.

Schneckloth v. Bustamonte, 412 U.S. 218, 93 S.Ct. 2041, 36 L.Ed.2d 854 (1973): Consent voluntarily given without coercion will permit a lawful search.

Stoner v. California, 376 U.S. 483, 84 S.Ct. 889, 11 L.Ed.2d 856 (1964): Only persons with actual or apparent authority over the premises may consent to a search of the premises.

Illinois v. Rodriguez, ___ U.S. ___, 110 S.Ct. 2793, 111 L.Ed.2d 148 (1990): The police may enter private premises without a warrant if they are acting in reliance upon the consent of a third party whom they reasonably, but mistakenly, believe has common authority over the premises.

Motor Vehicle Searches:

Carroll v. United States, 267 U.S. 132, 45 S.Ct. 280, 69 L.Ed. 543 (1925): A warrantless search of an automobile is permissible where there is probable cause to believe the vehicle may be carrying evidence or the fruits or instrumentalities of a crime.

Chambers v. Maroney, 399 U.S. 42, 90 S.Ct. 1975, 26 L.Ed.2d 419 (1970): Affirmed the right of officers to conduct a warrantless search of an arrested person's motor vehicle after it had been towed to the police station.

New York v. Belton, 453 U.S. 454, 101 S.Ct. 2860, 69 L.Ed. 2d 768 (1981): Incident to the lawful arrest of its occupant, the search of a vehicle's interior passenger compartment may include an examination of the contents of any closed or open containers, including the glove compartment, luggage, boxes, bags, clothing, or any other receptacles.

New York v. Class, 475 U.S. 106, 106 S.Ct. 960, 89 L.Ed.2d 81 (1986): There is no reasonable expectation of privacy in a vehicle identification number (VIN).

United States v. Ross, 456 U.S. 798, 102 S.Ct 2157, 72 L.Ed.2d. 572 (1982): A valid warrantless automobile search may, with probable cause, extend to the containers within the vehicle.

Plain View Doctrine

Horton v. California, 496 U.S. 128 110 S.Ct. 2301, 110 L.Ed.2d 112 (1990): A police officer may make a warrantless seizure of items whose character is "immediately apparent" regardless of whether he had prior reason to believe the items would be encountered. To justify warrantless seizure of an item in plain view, the police officer must not only be lawfully located in a place from which the object can be plainly seen, the officer must also have a lawful right or access to the object itself.

Coolidge v. New Hampshire, 403 U.S. 443, 91 S.Ct. 2022, 29 L.Ed.2d 564 (1971): A valid search warrant is re-

...ired to search a premises (dwelling) unless there are exi-
...ent circumstances. Plain view into a dwelling area is not
sufficient for a search.

Arizona v. Hicks, 480 U.S. 321, 107 S.Ct. 1149, 94
L.Ed.2d 347 (1987): Any movement of an object (e.g.,
turning over a piece of electronics to read its serial number)
is a "search" and does not come under the "plain view" exception to the warrant requirement.

Premises Searches

Bumper v. North Carolina, 391 U.S. 543, 88 S.Ct.
1788, 20 L.Ed.2d 797 (1968): A search where police gain
consensual admission to a premises through deception by
claiming to possess a warrant is unlawful.

California v. Greenwood, 486 U.S.35, 108 S.Ct. 1625
(1988): Placing garbage outside the curtilage (e.g., on the
curb or in a campground garbage can) results in a loss of a
reasonable expectation of privacy with respect to the contents.

United States v. Dunn, 480 U.S. 294, 107 S.Ct. 1134,
94 L.Ed.2d 326 (1987): The Court found four factors to be
considered when determining whether an area is within a
curtilage: (1) the proximity of the area to the home, (2)
whether the area is included in an enclosure around the
home, (3) the nature of uses to which area is put, and (4) the
steps taken by resident to protect the area from observation
by passersby.

United States v. Matlock, 415 U.S. 164, 94 S.Ct. 988,
39 L.Ed.2d 242 (1974): Any person with an equal right to a
premises may consent to a search of the premises.

Roadblocks

Michigan v. Sitz, ___ U.S. ___, 110 S.Ct. 2481, 110
L.Ed.2d 412 (1990): Police may employ highway checkpoint stops as a way of detecting and deterring motorists
who drive under the influence of intoxicants. Stopping and

briefly detaining all motorists passing through such che
points is constitutionally reasonable.

Searches Incident to Arrest

Chimel v. California: 395 U.S. 752, 89 S.Ct. 2034, 23
L.Ed.2d 685 (1969): Limited the scope of a search incident
to arrest to the area immediately around the arrestee ("jump
and reach" rule).

Hudson v. Palmer, 468 U.S. 517, 104 S.Ct. 3194, 82
L.Ed.2d 393 (1984): An incarcerated prisoner does not have
a reasonable expectation of privacy and is, therefore, not
protected by the Fourth Amendment's protection against unreasonable searches and seizures. A prisoner's clothes
could, therefore, be taken for examination, if the prisoner is
provided with replacement clothing.

Illinois v. Lafayette, 462 U.S. 640, 103 U.S. 2605, 77
L.Ed.2d 65 (1983): As a part of a routine procedure for admission to confinement, police may search the individual and
his or her personal effects if he or she is under lawful arrest.

United States v. Chadwick, 433 U.S. 1, 97 S.Ct.
2476, 53 L.Ed.2d 538 (1977): Sealed containers seized at
the time of arrest may not be searched without a warrant.

United States v. Edwards, 415 U.S. 800, 94 S.Ct.
1234, 39 L.Ed.2d 771 (1974): Pursuant to a lawful arrest,
clothing worn by the arrestee may be seized as evidence. The
arrestee must be given replacement clothing.

United States v. Robinson, 414 U.S. 218, 94 S.Ct.
467, 38 L.Ed.2d 427 (1973): In the case of a lawful, custodial arrest, a full search of the person and objects within his
possession is reasonable and proper without a warrant.

Vale v. Louisiana, 399 U.S. 30, 90 S.Ct. 1969, 26
L.Ed.2d 409 (1970): A warrantless search made incident to
arrest must be confined to the immediate vicinity of the arrest. (jump and reach rule).

vis v. Mississippi, 394 U.S. 721, 89 S.Ct. 1394, 22 .Ed.2d 676 (1969): Illegally seized evidence is inadmissible at trial.

Hayes v. Florida, 470 U.S. 811, 105 S.Ct. 1643, 84 L.Ed.2d 705 (1985): An individual's Fourth Amendment rights are violated when he is forcibly removed from a place he is entitled to be in order to obtain fingerprints, and the officers are acting without probable cause and judicial supervision.

Massachusetts v. Sheppard, 468 U.S. 981, 104 S.Ct. 3424, 82 L.Ed. 2d 737 (1984): When police officers take every reasonable step to obtain a valid search warrant from a detached, neutral magistrate who assures the officers of the warrant's validity, and when the officers proceed to enforce the warrant, acting in good faith, the evidence will be admissible even though the warrant is subsequently determined to be invalid.

United States v. Leon, 468 U.S. 897, 104 S.Ct. 3405, 82 L.Ed.2d 677 (1984): The Exclusionary Rule does not bar the use of evidence obtained by officers acting in good-faith reasonable reliance on a search warrant issued by a detached and neutral magistrate but ultimately found to be invalid.

Warden v. Hayden, 387 U.S. 294, 87 S.Ct. 1642, 18 L.Ed.2d 782 (1967): A search warrant is the means to search for specific items and does not provide access to a premises to shop for evidence to convict. The duration of the search is for the minimum time to discover the sought items.

Wong Sun v. United States, 371 U.S. 471, 83 S.Ct. 407, 9 L.Ed.2d 441 (1963): Evidence obtained through a lawful search, but based on illegally obtained information or evidence may be excluded as "fruit of the poisonous tree." If the connection between illegal police conduct and the challenged evidence is so removed in time and place or person so as to dissipate the taint, the evidence is admissible.

Warrantless Searches

Andresen v. Maryland, 427 U.S. 463, 96 S.Ct. 273, 49 L.Ed.2d 627 (1976): The Fifth Amendment protection against self incrimination attaches to the person not to information that may incriminate him.

Cupp v. Murphy, 412 U.S. 291, 93 S.Ct. 2000, 36 L.Ed.2d 900 (1973): Fingernail scrapings taken without consent and absent a formal arrest are constitutional.

Dunaway v. New York, 442 U.S. 200, 99 S.Ct. 2248, 60 L.Ed.2d 824 (1979): The Fourth Amendment is violated when a person is taken into custody, detained and questioned without probable cause. Evidence obtained from such a custodial questioning is inadmissible.

Minnesota v. Olson, 495 U.S. 91, 110 S.Ct. 1684, 109 L.Ed. 2d 85 (1990): A guest in a home has a legitimate expectation of privacy in the residence and is, therefore, entitled to the protection of the Fourth Amendment against police intrusion on that interest.

Schmerber v. California, 384 U.S. 757, 86 S.Ct. 1826, 16 L.Ed.2d 908 (1966): Where evidence in the blood could be destroyed by delay, a warrant is not necessary to take a blood sample. The Fifth Amendment prohibition on self incrimination applies only to items of a testimonial nature.

United States v. Dionisio, 410 U.S. 1, 93 S.Ct. 764, 35 L.Ed. 2d 67 (1973): Non-testimonial evidence is not protected by the Fourth Amendment's prohibition against unreasonable searches and seizures. Examples of non-testimonial evidence include such things as: fingerprinting, photographing, measurements, requests to write or speak for identification, stand, assume a stance, to engage in a particular task, make a particular gesture, or appear in a lineup.

STOP AND FRISK

Adams v. Williams, 407 U.S. 143, 92 S.Ct. 1921, 32 L.Ed.2d 612 (1972): An informant's tip may be sufficient a stop and frisk even though it would be inadequate to ~pport an arrest warrant. The officer must have a reason-~le belief that criminal activity is afoot and the informant's ~p must bear some indication of reliability.

Alabama v. White, ___ U.S. ___, 110 S. Ct. 2412, 110 L. Ed. 2d 301 (1990): The combination of an anonymous tip, which alleged that the defendant was about to transport cocaine in a car, and a police officer's corroboration of some of the tip's details provided reasonable suspicion for stopping the vehicle.

Brown v. Texas: 443 U.S. 47, 99 S.Ct. 2637, 61 L.Ed.2d 357 (1979): A person may not be forcibly stopped for mere suspicion. He may be stopped for reasonable (articulable) suspicion.

Terry v. Ohio: 392 U.S. 1, 88 S.Ct. 1868, 20 L.Ed.2d 889 (1968): Established the right of law enforcement officers to stop and frisk individuals whom they reasonably suspect of being involved in criminal activity and that they believe may be armed and dangerous.

United States v. Sharpe, 470 U.S. 675 105 S.Ct. 1568, 84 L.Ed.2d 605 (1985): A suspect may be detained for a brief period while officers conduct an investigation, provided the officers' actions are justified and limited to the needs under the circumstances.

SURVEILLANCE

California v. Ciraolo, 476 U.S. 207, 106 S.Ct. 1809, 90 L.Ed.2d 210 (1986): There is no reasonable expectation of privacy from aerial surveillance, even within a curtilage.

Oliver v. United States, 466 U.S. 170, 104 S.Ct. 1735, 80 L.Ed.2d 214 (1984): Open fields do not provide the setting for those intimate activities that the Fourth Amendment is intended to protect from governmental interference or surveillance. The Fourth Amendment does not protect merely subjective expectations of privacy, but only those expectations that society is prepared to recognize as reasonable.

THE CONSTITUTION OF THE UNITED STATES

SELECTED AMENDMENTS

from

THE BILL OF RIGHTS
(AMENDMENTS 1, 4, 5, 6, 8)

and the

FOURTEENTH AMENDMENT
SECTIONS 1 AND 5

AMENDMENT I

Congress shall make no law respecting an establishment of religion, or prohibiting the free exercise thereof; or abridging the freedom of speech, or of the press; or the right of the people peaceably to assemble, and to petition the Government for a redress of grievances.

. . . . .

AMENDMENT IV

The right of the people to be secure in their persons, houses, papers, and effects, against unreasonable searches and seizures, shall not be violated, and no Warrants shall issue, but upon probable cause, supported by Oath or affirmation, and particularly describing the place to be searched, and the persons or things to be seized.

AMENDMENT V

No person shall be held to answer for a capital, or otherwise infamous crime, unless on a presentment or indictment of a Grand Jury, except in cases arising in the land or naval forces, or in the Militia, when in actual service in time of War or public danger; nor shall any person be subject for the same offence to be twice put in jeopardy of life or limb; nor shall be compelled in any criminal case to be a witness

...st himself, nor be deprived of life, liberty, or property, ...out due process of law; nor shall private property be ...en for public use, without just compensation.

AMENDMENT VI

In all criminal prosecutions, the accused shall enjoy the right to a speedy and public trial, by an impartial jury of the State and district wherein the crime shall have been committed, which district shall have been previously ascertained by law, and to be informed of the nature and cause of the accusation; to be confronted with the witnesses against him; to have compulsory process for obtaining witnesses in his favor, and to have the Assistance of Counsel for his defence.

. . . . .

AMENDMENT VIII

Excessive bail shall not be required, nor excessive fines imposed, nor cruel and unusual punishments inflicted.

. . . . .

AMENDMENT XIV

Section 1. All persons born or naturalized in the United States, and subject to the jurisdiction thereof, are citizens of the United States and of the State wherein they reside. No State shall make or enforce any law which shall abridge the privileges or immunities of the citizens of the United States; nor shall any State deprive any person of life, liberty, or property, without due process of law; nor deny to any person within its jurisdiction the equal protection of the laws.

. . . . .

Section 5. The Congress shall have power to enforce, by appropriate legislation, the provisions of this article.

. . . . .

SELECTED PERTINENT STATUTES

from the

UNITED STATES CODE

18 U.S.C. §242 Deprivation of rights under color of law

Whoever, under color of any law, statute, ordinance, regulation, or custom, willfully subjects any inhabitant of any State, Territory or District to the deprivation of any rights, privileges, or immunities secured or protected by the Constitution or laws of the United States, or to different punishments, pains, or penalties, on account of such inhabitant being an alien, or by reason of his color, or race, than are prescribed for the punishment of citizens, shall be fined not more than $1,000 or imprisoned not more than one year, or both; and if death results shall be subject to imprisonment for any term of years or for life.

42 U.S.C. §1983 Civil action for deprivation of rights

Every person who, under color of any statute, ordinance, regulation, custom, or usage, of any State or Territory, subjects, or causes to be subjected, any citizen of the United States or other person within the jurisdiction thereof to the deprivation of any rights, privileges, or immunities secured by the Constitution and laws, shall be liable to the party injured in an action at law, suit in equity, or other proper proceeding for redress.

NOTES

186

NOTES